LETTING GO

Walking Away From A Toxic Relationships

Charles O. Brown

Table of Contents

PREFACE	1
Introduction	5
Recognizing Narcissism	9
Common Characteristics of Narcissists	10
Differences Between Healthy and Toxic Dynamics	13
Impact of Narcissistic Behavior on Partners	17
Final Thoughts	21
Biblical Guidance for Freedom	23
Principles of Liberation from Unhealthy Bonds	24
Scriptural Narratives for Inspiration	27
Balancing Faith and Personal Boundaries	31
Concluding Thoughts	34
Guard Your Heart	36
Identifying and Setting Boundaries	37
Guarding Against Manipulation	40
Cultivating Spiritual Resilience	44
Summary and Reflections	47
Understanding the Manipulation	49

- Recognizing Subtle Manipulation — 50
- Psychological Effects of Control — 52
- Biblical Stories of Manipulation — 55
- Final Insights — 58

Balancing Boundaries with Grace — 60
- Techniques for Effective Boundary Setting — 61
- Role of Forgiveness in Healing — 65
- Maintaining Grace Under Pressure — 68
- Final Thoughts — 72

Tools for Personal Growth — 74
- Journaling for Self-Discovery — 75
- Setting New Personal Goals — 79
- Embracing Community Support — 82
- Concluding Thoughts — 86

Stories of Triumph — 88
- Transformative Personal Stories — 89
- Lessons Learned from Adversity — 92
- Inspirational Biblical Comparisons — 95
- Final Thoughts — 98

Restoration and Forgiveness — 100
- Steps to Personal Reconciliation — 101
- Finding Strength in Vulnerability — 105
- Role of Forgiveness in Self-Healing — 108
- Final Thoughts — 112

Walking Away with God — 114

Embracing New Life Chapters	115
Building a Stronger Faith Foundation	119
Lessons of Love and Loss Through Scripture	123
Final Insights	127
Conclusion	129
Reference Page	134
Letting Go: Walking Away from Toxic Relationships	134
Chapter 1 - Recognizing Narcissism	134
My Other books	151

Chapter One
PREFACE

In the tapestry of human experience, relationships stand as one of the most intricate and defining threads. They have the power to uplift, heal, and inspire, yet they can also wound, diminish, and confine. For those entangled in the web of narcissistic relationships, the struggle is profoundly isolating and emotionally draining. This book, "Letting Go: Walking Away from Toxic Relationships," is both a guide and a companion for anyone seeking clarity, liberation, and healing.

The journey of understanding and breaking free from toxic dynamics is neither straightforward nor easy. Often, the manipulative and controlling behaviors characteristic of narcissistic relationships are subtle, deeply ingrained, and shrouded in emotional complexities. Victims may find themselves questioning their reality, their self-worth, and even their faith. This book seeks to illuminate a path out of this darkness by providing a blend of practical strategies, personal reflections, and spiritual insights.

At its core, "Letting Go" emphasizes the transformative power of faith. Drawing on biblical wisdom, it offers a framework for recognizing unhealthy patterns, setting boundaries, and rediscovering one's God-given identity and purpose. Each chapter is designed to build on the last, creating a comprehensive roadmap for navigating the challenges of toxic relationships while anchoring oneself in the unwavering truths of scripture.

This book begins with understanding—an exploration of the characteristics of narcissistic individuals and the dynamics they create in relationships. By delving into the traits and tactics of narcissists, readers are equipped with the knowledge to identify red flags and confront uncomfortable truths. This awareness is the first step toward reclaiming one's autonomy and emotional health.

Faith plays a central role in this journey, and "Letting Go" is steeped in the wisdom of scripture. From the liberation narratives of the Israelites to the teachings of Jesus, the Bible provides timeless principles for breaking free from oppression and walking in the light of truth and love. The book weaves these teachings into practical guidance, offering readers actionable steps to integrate faith with personal boundaries and emotional resilience.

The chapters on boundary-setting and spiritual resilience are particularly vital. Setting boundaries is not merely about keeping others out but about creating a safe space where healing and growth can flourish.

This involves clear communication, self-awareness, and a commitment to preserving one's peace. Similarly, cultivating spiritual resilience provides the strength to endure challenges, find solace in prayer and community, and maintain hope amidst adversity.

The stories of triumph included in this book serve as powerful reminders that freedom is not only possible but also profoundly rewarding. These narratives, drawn from both biblical accounts and modern experiences, showcase the resilience of the human spirit and the redemptive power of faith. They are a testament to the fact that no matter how deep the scars, healing and restoration are within reach.

"Letting Go" is not just for those directly impacted by toxic relationships. It is also a valuable resource for counselors, pastors, and support group leaders who walk alongside individuals on their journeys to freedom. By combining psychological insights with biblical truths, this book equips helpers with the tools to provide compassionate and effective support.

As you embark on this journey through the pages of "Letting Go," may you find hope, encouragement, and empowerment. Whether you are seeking to break free yourself or to guide someone else toward healing, let this book be a source of inspiration and strength. Remember, freedom is not just the absence of oppression but the presence of peace, purpose, and divine love. You are not alone, and with faith as your anchor, the path to liberation is illuminated by grace and truth.

Chapter Two
Introduction

In the theater of relationships, there are acts that unfold so beautifully they seem almost scripted by a divine hand. The laughter shared, the support given, the warmth of loving arms that seems to reassure us with every embrace—all these create moments so perfect, they make us believe in fairy tales. Yet, sometimes, beneath this serene facade lurks an undercurrent of manipulation and control, a hidden world where smiles mask deceit and affection is replaced with possession. Have you ever found yourself ensnared in such a dichotomy, caught between the apparent perfection and an insidious reality? This book, "Letting Go," dives into the tumultuous waves of these complex relationships, offering a lighthouse of hope and guidance for those navigating these stormy seas.

"Letting Go" is crafted for two groups of travelers on this challenging journey. First, it speaks directly to those who find themselves ensnared in toxic relationships, yearning for validation, healing, and the courage to seek a healthier path. If you're feeling trapped, questioning your worth each day, and carrying the weight of emotional scars, this book reaches out to you with compassion and understanding. It seeks to reinforce what you may have forgotten—that your value is intrinsic and your spirit deserving of liberation and love. You are not alone in this struggle. Many souls have embarked on similar paths of turmoil and emerged stronger, guided by a wisdom greater than any earthly challenge.

The second audience this book aims to serve includes Christian counselors and support group leaders. As beacons of hope within communities, you offer essential support and guidance to individuals seeking refuge from toxic environments. "Letting Go" provides resources to bolster your efforts, weaving together biblical teachings with practical insights to aid others in reclaiming their lives from the grip of destructive relationships. By equipping you with these tools, we hope to empower you to continue fostering healing and resilience within your communities, illuminating paths toward peace and growth for those who seek it.

The foundation of our journey lies in the powerful interplay between faith and personal strength. The sacred texts have long spoken to the trials of the human soul, offering solace and direction amidst chaos. Within these pages, you'll discover how God's truths can guide you through recognizing harmful patterns and rebuilding your life with renewed purpose and empowerment. By intertwining scriptural wisdom and personal narratives, we aim to build bridges over turbulent waters—a way forward illuminated by both faith and understanding.

Our quest begins with recognition. To break free from toxicity, one must first see it for what it truly is. This means stripping away the illusions and confronting the uncomfortable truths. We delve into identifying narcissistic behaviors and toxic traits that often masquerade as love, helping you discern red flags that might otherwise remain unseen. Through this enlightenment, you will learn that acknowledging the problem is not a reflection of weakness but the first step toward regaining control over your life.

With awareness comes the need for boundaries—an essential aspect of preserving one's mental and spiritual well-being. Boundaries serve as protective barriers against further harm, empowering you to stand firm in your convictions while maintaining your peace. We explore how to establish and uphold these limits, drawing inspiration from biblical examples of steadfastness in the face of adversity. Just as Nehemiah rebuilt the walls of Jerusalem, you too can fortify your soul against external assaults, creating a safe haven for growth and healing.

Healing is a central theme woven throughout our narrative. Emotional and spiritual restoration requires time, patience, and, often, community. Here, we share transformative personal stories of those who have traveled this rocky path before you—stories that echo with pain yet resonate with triumph. These narratives are reminders that while the journey may be arduous, it is also profoundly rewarding. In sharing these experiences, we strive to inspire hope and healing in your heart, encouraging you to embrace the process of recovery fully.

Practical tools round out our exploration, offering tangible steps to implement changes in your everyday life. From journaling exercises designed to foster self-reflection to affirmations that reinforce your self-worth, these resources are meant to equip you for the challenges ahead. As you progress through "Letting Go," these tools will become invaluable companions, guiding you toward a future defined by strength and serenity.

Ultimately, "Letting Go" is more than just a guide; it's an invitation—to rediscover your identity, rekindle your faith, and reclaim a life unburdened by the chains of toxic relationships. As you turn each page, we hope you find encouragement and empowerment, knowing that the road to freedom is lined with blessings and grace. May this journey lead you to a place of profound healing and unwavering hope, where your spirit can soar free and unfettered once more.

Chapter Three
Recognizing Narcissism

Recognizing narcissism is a journey that involves understanding the subtle yet profound impact of narcissistic behaviors within relationships. Many people enter relationships with dreams of mutual love and understanding, only to find themselves questioning their reality amidst a whirlwind of confusion and self-doubt. The intricate dance of narcissism captivates individuals into a cycle where admiration turns into exploitation, leaving partners feeling eternally inadequate. While it can be tempting to overlook or excuse these manipulative tendencies in the context of love, the consequences often manifest as emotional scars that necessitate healing and reflection. This awareness, however unsettling, marks the initial step towards reclaiming one's agency and reconnecting with an authentic sense of self-worth.

This chapter delves into the world of narcissistic traits and their unmistakable presence in relationships. Readers will explore various characteristics such as the unquenchable need for attention, lack of empathy, manipulative strategies like gaslighting, and the pervasive sense of entitlement that define such interactions. Each characteristic serves as a red flag, signaling broader patterns of behavior that often lead to one-sided and toxic dynamics. Understanding these traits empowers readers not just to identify them but to recognize their insidious nature before they overshadow personal well-being. By shedding light on these traits, the chapter provides guidance for both individuals seeking liberation from toxic relationships and those aiming to support others on their path to healing. Through this knowledge, readers are equipped to confront the challenges posed by narcissism and take meaningful steps toward nurturing healthier connections anchored in mutual respect and empathy.

Common Characteristics of Narcissists

Identifying narcissistic behavior in relationships can be challenging, yet recognizing these traits is essential for both personal awareness and self-protection. Narcissism often manifests through a set of easily identifiable behaviors, primarily rooted in an excessive need for admiration, a lack of empathy, manipulative tactics, and a sense of entitlement.

One of the most prominent characteristics of narcissistic individuals is their insatiable need for admiration and validation. This requirement often comes with demanding constant attention from their partners or loved ones. In such a dynamic, they may continuously seek praise for their achievements or appearance, frequently turning conversations back to themselves. This focus on their self-image without considering others' needs leads to imbalanced relationships, where the narcissistic person becomes the central figure. Partners may feel pressured to constantly provide affirmation, leaving little room for their own needs to be addressed (Smith & Robinson, 2018).

Moreover, a noticeable lack of empathy is a core component of narcissistic behavior. Individuals who exhibit this trait often struggle to genuinely connect with the emotions of others. They tend to dismiss their partner's concerns, seeing them as insignificant compared to their own. This emotional neglect breeds confusion and isolation, as partners may begin to doubt their worth or question if their feelings are valid. The absence of empathetic understanding fosters an environment where honest and open emotional exchanges are rare, hampering the development of true intimacy and support (Ronningstam, 2023).

Manipulative behavior is another significant hallmark of narcissism, particularly seen through tactics like gaslighting. Gaslighting involves manipulating someone into questioning their reality, memories, or perceptions. This form of psychological manipulation serves to undermine the partner's confidence and perspective. For example, a narcissistic individual might consistently deny their hurtful actions or minimize their partner's feelings, suggesting that they are overreacting or imagining things. This erosion of trust in one's own judgment can be deeply damaging, making it difficult for individuals to rely on their instincts or interpretations of situations. It's a tactic that reinforces dependency on the narcissist, as the victim becomes unsure of themselves and leans more on the manipulator for cues about what is real (Smith & Robinson, 2018).

Although not every act of manipulation is immediately evident, patterns already mentioned can serve as warning signals. It's critical to remain vigilant and recognize these signs as red flags in any relationship.

Finally, entitlement in narcissistic individuals often results in one-sided relationships characterized by exploitation and unjust demands. A sense of superiority propels them to prioritize their desires over those of their partner. This could manifest as expecting special treatment or assuming the right to control decisions within the relationship without consulting the partner. Such behaviors can lead to an environment where the partner feels inadequate, trapped under the weight of the narcissist's expectations and demeaning behavior. This entitlement reveals itself through repeated instances where the narcissist's needs are met at the expense of their partner's well-being, leading to an unequal distribution of power and respect (Ronningstam, 2023).

Differences Between Healthy and Toxic Dynamics

In the intricate realm of relationships, discerning between healthy and toxic dynamics becomes a crucial endeavor. Understanding these distinctions not only aids in fostering stronger bonds but also helps individuals safeguard their emotional well-being.

Open communication serves as a cornerstone of healthy relationships, creating an environment where individuals feel free to express their thoughts and emotions. In such settings, partners engage in discussions that build understanding and trust, ensuring both parties feel heard and valued. For instance, if disagreements arise, healthy couples are more likely to address issues directly, tackling misunderstandings head-on rather than allowing them to fester. The practice of open dialogue cultivates a shared connection, reducing the likelihood of resentment or unresolved conflicts.

Conversely, toxic relationships often resort to the silent treatment as a means of control or punishment, creating an atmosphere thick with tension and uncertainty. This form of communication—or lack thereof—instills fear and doubt, leaving individuals walking on eggshells, unsure of when or if issues will be addressed. The absence of open communication in these contexts breeds isolation and insecurity, detracting from the relationship's potential for growth.

Mutual respect stands as another pillar of healthy relationship dynamics, contributing significantly to personal and collective growth. When partners regard each other with respect, they nurture a space where ideas can flourish, and differences are celebrated rather than criticized. Respect is shown through actions and words, reinforcing a partner's self-worth and confidence. It encourages one another to pursue personal goals, providing reassurance and support along the way.

On the opposite end of the spectrum, constant criticism in toxic relationships erodes self-esteem, leading to a lingering sense of inadequacy. Rather than feeling supported, individuals may find themselves persistently undermined, with every action scrutinized and dismissed. This barrage of negativity strips away confidence, often resulting in feelings of worthlessness and helplessness. Such dynamics trap individuals in cycles of self-doubt, hampering personal development and fostering dependency on their partner for validation.

Supportive relationships further exemplify the nurturing nature of healthy connections, where each partner actively encourages the other's aspirations and celebrates successes. This mutual reinforcement of goals and dreams creates a partnership grounded in positivity and optimism. In these environments, recognizing each other's achievements galvanizes both partners to strive for more, making joint progress toward shared and individual objectives.

In stark contrast, toxic relationships are marked by sabotage and obstruction, where one partner may undermine the other's ambitions, either overtly or subtly. This destructive behavior can manifest as discouragement, ridicule, or manipulation, designed to stifle the partner's potential and maintain control. The resulting effect is a relationship where one person diminishes the other, preventing them from reaching their full capabilities and leaving them marooned in mediocrity.

Flexibility plays a significant role in healthy relationships, promoting collaboration and negotiation between partners. When flexibility is present, couples can work through challenges and adapt to change more readily. This adaptability allows for the evolution of the relationship itself, accommodating shifts in lifestyle, goals, and preferences over time. The ability to compromise and adjust strengthens the bond, ensuring it remains resilient and dynamic in the face of life's unpredictabilities.

However, rigidity typifies toxic relationships, wherein one or both partners may exhibit inflexibility around expectations or roles. This unyielding attitude creates a sense of entrapment, as individuals find themselves confined within restrictive boundaries that leave no room for growth or personal autonomy. Such constraints hinder the natural progression of the relationship, leading to frustration and resentment. Over time, this stagnation fosters an environment where true closeness is impossible, as freedom and individuality are suppressed for the sake of maintaining control or avoiding conflict.

In navigating these contrasting dynamics, it becomes clear that healthy relationships thrive on a foundation of openness, respect, support, and flexibility. These components empower individuals and partnerships alike, paving the way for fulfilling and enriching experiences. In contrast, toxic relationships rely on silence, criticism, sabotage, and rigidity, all of which corrode the foundations of trust and love.

Acknowledging these distinctions enables individuals to make informed choices about their relationships, equipping them with the insights needed to foster healthier, more supportive interactions moving forward.

Understanding these dynamics can not only transform personal relationships but also extend to assisting others in similar situations. By recognizing toxic patterns, individuals can seek necessary change, whether through personal reflection, open dialogue with their partner, or pursuing external support. Cultivating a mindset that values mutual respect, open communication, positive reinforcement, and adaptability ensures a nurturing environment where all parties can flourish. With these insights and practices in mind, the path to healthier relationship dynamics becomes attainable, encouraging growth, happiness, and fulfillment.

Impact of Narcissistic Behavior on Partners

In the shadows of a relationship marked by narcissism, partners often face emotional turmoil that can be deeply damaging. The effects are multifaceted, ranging from diminished self-esteem to overwhelming confusion. Navigating life while emotionally entangled with a narcissistic partner can leave profound scars on one's mental and emotional well-being.

One of the most insidious impacts of narcissistic behavior is the erosion of self-esteem. A narcissistic partner tends to bombard their loved ones with belittling remarks and criticisms, chipping away at their confidence bit by bit. This constant stream of negative messages can lead an individual to internalize these harmful beliefs, resulting in a significant loss of self-worth. It's akin to being trapped in a cycle where you begin to see yourself through the unforgiving lens of your partner's criticism. Over time, this relentless barrage not only lowers self-esteem but also instills a belief that one is not deserving of respect or kindness. These feelings of inadequacy become ingrained, making it difficult for the affected person to envision a world where they are valued and appreciated. Understanding this dynamic and recognizing these demeaning patterns is crucial to breaking free from such toxic relationships (Fishman, 2017).

Chronic stress and anxiety are other inevitable outcomes of enduring narcissistic abuse. The unpredictability of reactions from a narcissistic partner creates an environment of constant alertness. Living under such conditions is mentally exhausting, as the partner must constantly anticipate how any action or word might provoke a negative response. This perpetual state of readiness takes a toll, leading to heightened stress levels and anxiety. Imagine living each day on edge, never knowing when the next storm will hit. This kind of psychological pressure can manifest as panic attacks, insomnia, or even physical ailments—responses to stress that linger long after the immediate threat has passed. It's like walking through life expecting an earthquake at every turn, where even moments of calm are fraught with tension. Supportive interventions, like therapy, can help unravel these tightly wound nerves, providing individuals with tools to manage and eventually overcome anxiety induced by such unpredictable dynamics.

Isolation is another devastating result of involvement with a narcissist. Narcissists often work to sever their partner's connections to supportive networks, whether friends, family, or colleagues. Through manipulation and control, they create rifts between their partner and these important emotional supports, leaving them feeling alone and dependent solely on the narcissist. This isolation serves to deepen the partner's dependency, as they have fewer outlets for emotional support or alternative perspectives on their situation. It is a calculated tactic to strengthen the narcissistic partner's hold over them. By alienating them from those who care about them, the victim finds it increasingly challenging to reach out for help or see a way out. The loneliness can be suffocating, a silent agreement that spirals into an unhealthy reliance on the very person causing harm. Rebuilding these connections is vital. Engaging in community activities or seeking counseling can provide new avenues for interaction and support, helping break the cycle of isolation.

Confusion and self-doubt are also common consequences, born from the unpredictable nature of life with a narcissist. Narcissists excel at gaslighting—a form of manipulation that forces their partners to question their own perceptions and feelings. Through this psychological tactic, they deny past events or alter reality, leaving their partner feeling uncertain and disoriented. Such confusion leads to a persistent state of self-doubt, as individuals find themselves questioning their judgment and sanity. This distortion of reality traps them in a fog where truth feels elusive and their voice subdued. The unpredictability makes them second-guess every emotion, transforming clarity into a tangled web of doubt. Overcoming the confusion requires re-establishing trust in one's perceptions and emotions, potentially with the help of professional guidance to reaffirm what is real and adjust to healthier thought patterns (Cuncic, 2021).

Establishing guidelines for moving forward involves building resilience against these patterns. With diminutive self-esteem, it is beneficial to regularly engage in affirmations or therapy sessions focused on self-worth reconstruction. For those facing isolation, intentionally reaching out to regain lost connections or forming new friendships can provide the strength needed to disengage from the narcissist. When dealing with confusion and self-doubt, keeping a journal of experiences and emotions can validate what happened and clarify feelings, serving as a reference point amid the chaos. Additionally, adopting a flexible mindset towards healing rather than rigid expectations can enable individuals to adapt and thrive beyond the confines of their past ordeals.

Final Thoughts

Navigating the complexities of relationships with individuals who exhibit narcissistic traits can often feel overwhelming and exhausting. This chapter sheds light on identifying these behaviors, equipping readers with the knowledge needed to recognize and understand their impact. The excessive need for admiration, lack of empathy, manipulative tactics, and a sense of entitlement are not mere quirks but significant indicators of narcissism that cultivate environments of imbalance and control. By acknowledging these patterns, individuals in such relationships can begin to realize how much they've been shaped by the demands and neglect characteristic of narcissistic dynamics. Recognizing these signs is the first step towards regaining personal autonomy and emotional clarity.

Empathy remains our guiding light as we reflect on the effects of narcissistic behavior. The steady erosion of self-esteem, increased stress and anxiety levels, and diminishing connections with supportive networks leave partners feeling confused and isolated. These emotional wounds, though deep, are not beyond healing. If you find yourself in such a situation, remember that understanding these dynamics provides a path to change. Seeking support from friends, counselors, or faith communities can be invaluable. As we move forward, embracing a healing mindset through small steps like reaching out, documenting emotions, and affirming self-worth is crucial. With courage and perseverance, you can rebuild, restore your sense of self, and foster healthier, more fulfilling relationships.

Chapter Four
Biblical Guidance for Freedom

Understanding biblical guidance for freedom is about delving into the spiritual wisdom that helps us break free from toxic relationships. The scriptures offer profound insights into the essence of freedom, portraying it as a divine gift meant to enhance personal growth and harmonious living. In a world where unhealthy ties can cloud our lives, these teachings provide clarity and encouragement. They guide us to recognize when a relationship becomes harmful, teaching us to prioritize environments that nurture rather than diminish our well-being. This journey requires courage and discernment, with faith serving as a compass towards healthier bonds. The Bible encourages us to reflect on our connections, offering tools to identify and overcome the emotional chains that may bind us, all within the comforting embrace of God's love and wisdom.

As you read this chapter, you will explore the rich tapestry of biblical principles that illuminate paths to liberation from toxic relationships. We delve into scripture to reveal its role in highlighting the need for freedom and recognizing toxicity's signs. You'll discover how certain verses guide individuals in setting and maintaining effective boundaries without compromising spiritual integrity. The chapter unfolds narratives of hope and transformation found within the Bible, showcasing stories of deliverance that serve as beacons of possibility and strength. Additionally, the supportive role of community is examined, emphasizing the collective power in fostering healing and providing refuge. Practical steps grounded in faith are shared, encouraging actionable change while leaning on divine promises of restoration and peace. Through these discussions, readers are invited to embark on or continue their journey toward liberation, supported by biblical wisdom and compassionate understanding.

Principles of Liberation from Unhealthy Bonds

Understanding how scripture guides liberation from toxicity is a profound journey that intertwines spiritual wisdom with personal growth. The Bible offers a wealth of guidance on the essence of freedom, emphasizing it as a divine right essential for pursuing healthy relationships and a life characterized by peace. This perspective is grounded in the belief that God desires His people to thrive in environments that nurture rather than harm them.

Biblical verses underscore the importance of freedom, clearly signaling that individuals are meant to live in harmony and not under the bondage of toxic relationships. Scriptures such as 2 Corinthians 3:17 state, "Where the Spirit of the Lord is, there is freedom." This freedom is not only from sin but also from oppressive ties that distort our sense of self and well-being. Understanding this liberty allows individuals to pursue bonds that reflect God's love and peace, reinforcing their journey towards healthier interactions.

Discerning unhealthy relationships through scripture provides a powerful lens to identify harmful behaviors and dynamics. For example, Galatians 5:19-21 lists traits like jealousy, fits of rage, and discord as works of the flesh, contrasting them with the fruits of the Spirit, which include love, joy, and peace (Galatians 5:22-23). By examining our relationships against these qualities, we gain clarity on whether they align with the life-giving principles of Scripture. Toxicity can manifest as control, manipulation, or emotional turmoil, which are contrary to the biblical vision of love and support. Recognizing these patterns is the first step towards breaking free and seeking positive change.

The role of community in providing essential support for healing cannot be overstated. Engaging with a community that embodies friendship, accountability, and shared experiences is crucial in overcoming toxic ties. Ecclesiastes 4:9-10 expresses this beautifully: "Two are better than one... If either of them falls down, one can help the other up." Being part of a supportive network offers encouragement and strength, creating a safe space for healing and growth. As you navigate the complexities of leaving a toxic relationship, each member of your community plays a vital role in offering comfort, prayer, and practical help, reinforcing that you are not alone on this path.

A guideline to consider is actively participating in group meetings or church activities that emphasize collective support. Christian groups often provide structured environments where shared stories and mutual understanding foster deeper connections. Regular involvement in such communities helps maintain focus on spiritual growth while ensuring emotional support is readily available. Engaging with fellow believers who have trodden similar paths can offer insights and hope, proving invaluable in the journey toward liberation.

Moreover, assurance that God's promises include restoration and healing is fundamental for those pursuing freedom from toxic ties. The narrative of Job reminds us of God's restorative power. After enduring immense suffering, God restored Job's fortunes, signifying that He can bring wholeness even after deep wounds. The Bible reassures us that despite the challenges faced, God is invested in our healing and future.

Jeremiah 29:11 further emphasizes this promise, declaring: "For I know the plans I have for you...plans to prosper you and not to harm you, plans to give you hope and a future." This verse provides solace, reminding us that God's intentions are rooted in prosperity and hope rather than harm. Through prayer and meditation on these scriptures, believers can find courage and faith to seek out new beginnings, confident in the knowledge that God champions their journey towards freedom.

Scriptural Narratives for Inspiration

Gaining inspiration from biblical stories for freedom can offer profound insights and hope to individuals yearning for liberation from toxic relationships. In the Bible, stories of deliverance provide a vivid illustration of God's active intervention in liberating people from adverse situations. These narratives serve as potent reminders that divine help is available to those who seek it with faith and courage.

One compelling example is the story of the Israelites' exodus from Egypt, a powerful account of deliverance where God leads His people out of slavery into freedom. This narrative exemplifies how faith in God and persistence lead to liberation, even when faced with apparently insurmountable challenges. The Israelites, oppressed under Pharaoh's rule, were granted freedom through a series of miraculous events orchestrated by God. This story not only highlights God's power but also demonstrates that deliverance often requires taking bold steps and placing unwavering trust in a higher power.

The Bible invites us to take action, aligning our efforts with divine will. Faith without action remains stagnant, but when combined, they become a formidable force for change. The courage to leave a toxic relationship, setting boundaries, or seeking support reflects an alignment with biblical principles. Such actions resonate with the encouragement found in Philippians 1:6, which reassures believers that God, who began a good work within them, will carry it on to completion. Recognizing the need for practical steps in the journey towards freedom aligns with this message and encourages taking decisive measures while trusting in

God's ongoing work in one's life (Freedom & Transformation Archives - Maryann Ward, 2024).

Paul's epistles are another rich source of guidance on navigating relational challenges according to God's values. Through his letters, Paul emphasizes love, compassion, and forgiveness—qualities essential for healthy relationships. In Ephesians, Paul writes about growing together in love, indicating that mutual respect and understanding must be foundational elements in any relationship. His advice guides us toward nurturing relationships that reflect God's love rather than perpetuating harm or toxicity.

Incorporating these teachings into real-life scenarios, individuals can reassess their relationships through the lens of biblical values. Paul's emphasis on embodying Christ-like qualities serves as a reminder to approach each interaction with patience and kindness. When conflicts arise, responding with love rather than retaliation aligns with the directives given in his writings. By embedding these virtues into daily interactions, believers can foster environments of trust and mutual respect, distancing themselves from toxic patterns.

Faith and action, as demonstrated in various biblical stories, provide a framework for approaching personal struggles with inspired resolution. The narrative of David and Goliath, for instance, encapsulates the spirit of confronting one's giants with faith-fueled action. David's reliance on God, paired with his boldness to act against Goliath, showcases the potential victories attainable through faith-driven action. This aligns with biblical examples and empowers readers to take practical steps towards overcoming obstacles, including those presented by harmful relationships. Developing a discernment that balances faith and tangible steps can guide individuals in creating a path free from toxicity.

Miraculous transformations within scripture further amplify the hope for change and renewal. Consider the conversion of Saul to Paul, one of the most dramatic transformations recorded in the New Testament. Saul, a known persecutor of Christians, encounters Jesus on the road to Damascus, leading to a complete spiritual overhaul. His transformation from antagonist to apostle illustrates the profound changes that faith can inspire. Such narratives provide assurance to readers facing similar trials, confirming that no situation is beyond redemption. Trusting in divine intervention and embracing the possibility of personal transformation can be a cornerstone for those seeking escape from detrimental relationships.

Hope shines brightly in the potential for miracles, both large and small, in our lives. While these biblical accounts may seem extraordinary, they echo the truth that significant change is feasible through perseverance and faith. Romans 12:2 underscores this notion, urging believers to embrace new perspectives and abandon worldly customs in favor of transformative renewal. Whether it's gaining the strength to leave a toxic relationship or finding peace amidst chaos, these acts of faith echo the miraculous changes seen throughout scripture (From Desperation to Transformation, 2020).

Balancing Faith and Personal Boundaries

In navigating the complex terrain of relationships, establishing personal boundaries is an essential practice advocated by biblical teachings. The Bible provides a framework for setting these boundaries to maintain relational health and protect our well-being. In Proverbs 4:23, we find wisdom in "guarding your heart," which highlights the importance of maintaining personal integrity and emotional health. God's word emphasizes the need for discernment and careful evaluation of relationships to avoid harmful influences (Leight, 2021). By setting limits that align with divine guidance, individuals safeguard their spiritual, mental, and emotional states, ultimately supporting healthier interactions.

Practical application of faith plays a crucial role in setting boundaries with empathy. It's not merely about drawing lines but doing so in a way that preserves love while upholding one's values and integrity. Ephesians 4:15 encourages believers to speak the truth in love, demonstrating that boundaries should be communicated kindly and clearly. This balance between love and truth prevents enabling unhealthy patterns, as enabling could lead to deeper harm. When Jesus interacted with others, he consistently demonstrated boundaries that were firm yet compassionate, exemplifying how one can love others without compromising personal values (*How Healthy Boundaries Are More about God and Other People (Not Me)*, 2024).

Healthy boundaries are also instrumental in fostering spiritual growth. They are not simply defensive mechanisms; rather, they nurture self-respect and improve relationships by creating environments where mutual respect and understanding thrive. Boundaries allow each person to grow individually while contributing positively to relationships. For instance, when someone respects another's need for time and space, it fosters personal development and reflects respect for their journey. Such an approach recognizes the divinely instilled worth within every individual, encouraging them to explore their potential fully.

While it's crucial to set boundaries, trusting God during this process aligns decisions with His divine will. This trust provides reassurance and confidence, especially in difficult transitions. Philippians 4:6-7 advises believers to present their requests to God with thanksgiving, promising peace that surpasses understanding. By surrendering boundary-setting processes to God, individuals experience divine wisdom guiding their actions (Leight, 2021). This assurance strengthens their resolve, knowing that their choices reflect God's desires for their lives, even when facing challenges.

However, setting boundaries requires practical steps as mentioned above. Seeking guidance through prayer and scripture study helps believers gain clarity on appropriate boundary measures. It is important to communicate these boundaries assertively yet lovingly, ensuring that intentions are understood by all involved. Engaging in open dialogue with trusted support systems—such as church communities or counselors—provides additional perspectives and encouragement. Finally, remaining flexible and willing to adjust boundaries as situations evolve is vital to ensure they remain relevant and effective in preserving relational health.

The establishment of healthy boundaries transcends mere personal protection, aiming instead to glorify God through maintaining the dignity, empathy, and compassion that Jesus himself exhibited. Christians are called not only to consider their needs but to maintain an outward focus, ensuring that their actions mirror Christ's example.

Concluding Thoughts

This chapter explored the deep wisdom found in scripture regarding liberation from toxic relationships, emphasizing that freedom is a divine right and essential for living a life of peace. Through various biblical verses, we've seen how God calls us to recognize harmful patterns and seek healthier interactions rooted in love and peace. Understanding these scriptural principles empowers individuals to discern and break free from ties that distort their well-being. The role of community support, highlighted in this exploration, is vital. It acts as a reassuring pillar during the challenging process of leaving behind toxicity. Shared experiences and mutual encouragement within such communities provide the strength needed to move forward.

As we reflect on these teachings, it becomes clear that balancing faith and action is crucial in overcoming relational challenges. The stories of deliverance from the Bible remind us to act with courage and trust in

God's ongoing work in our lives. Setting personal boundaries, as guided by scripture, ensures we maintain emotional and spiritual health while fostering respectful relationships. The journey towards freedom is not walked alone; it is supported by faith, community, and intentional steps. Embracing these elements allows us to live out God's plan for healing and hope, cultivating an environment where love and respect can thrive.

Chapter Five
Guard Your Heart

Guarding your heart is an essential practice in navigating the complexities of emotional and spiritual well-being. It involves a conscious effort to protect oneself from harmful influences and preserve inner peace. Many people find themselves worn out by toxic relationships or overwhelmed by manipulative behaviors, feeling trapped in cycles that drain their emotional energy. Understanding how to safeguard this personal sanctuary can be transformative, providing both clarity and strength. As you embark on this journey, it's important to recognize the significance of setting boundaries, cultivating resilience, and allowing yourself to grow beyond present limitations.

This chapter delves into practical strategies to shield your heart from external pressures. You'll explore the art of establishing personal boundaries and recognizing manipulation's subtle signs, empowering you to trust your instincts when confronted with unsettling dynamics. Additionally, developing spiritual resilience becomes a guiding force, enabling you to find solace and strength through faith and community. By nurturing these aspects within yourself, you'll learn not only to withstand challenges but to thrive in the midst of them. The insights shared herein aim to equip you with the tools needed to foster healing and encouragement in both personal journeys and communal settings, ultimately leading to a more robust emotional and spiritual life.

Identifying and Setting Boundaries

In the journey toward safeguarding our emotional health, understanding personal limits serves as a foundational step. Establishing personal boundaries is essential for maintaining emotional and physical well-being, empowering individuals to advocate for themselves. Personal boundaries define the space we are comfortable with emotionally, physically, and spiritually. They act as a protective barrier that accentuates self-respect and ensures that one's needs and values are honored (Katherine, 2010).

To begin with, understanding personal limits means being aware of what makes you uncomfortable or stressed in various situations. This self-awareness helps to navigate interactions and relationships effectively. For instance, if you find yourself consistently drained after spending time with certain people, it's a signal to assess your boundaries. Recognizing these signs allows you to prioritize your mental well-being by choosing when and how to engage in relationships that affect your peace of mind.

Communicating boundaries effectively is crucial once you've identified your personal limits. Clear communication minimizes misunderstandings and fosters respect from others, making relationship dynamics healthier. Openly expressing your boundaries isn't about demanding but rather asserting your needs respectfully. When conveyed assertively, boundaries become a form of self-care that teaches others how to treat us (Nash, 2018). For example, stating, "I need some personal time each week to recharge," sets a clear expectation without room for misinterpretation.

Effective communication involves using 'I' statements that focus on your feelings rather than criticizing the other's behavior. For instance, instead of saying, "You never listen to me," try "I feel unheard when I am interrupted." This approach encourages constructive dialogue and reduces defensive reactions. Practicing such communication can initially be challenging, especially for those who have spent years neglecting their needs due to external pressures or codependency issues. However, it gradually becomes easier with practice and patience (Reid, 2022).

Evaluating relationship impact is another critical aspect of boundary setting. Regularly assessing your relationships helps recognize any negative impacts they might have on your emotional well-being, guiding where boundaries need to be set or adjusted. Consider asking yourself: Does this relationship drain my energy? Do I feel valued and respected? These reflections provide clarity and aid in deciding which relationships nurture growth and which may require re-evaluation or stronger boundaries.

An important component of this evaluation process is recognizing patterns that might signify unhealthy dynamics, such as manipulation, frequent disrespect, or constant emotional exhaustion. Identifying these red flags enables you to make informed decisions about how to handle such relationships moving forward. It empowers you to take action in creating a healthier, more balanced life where your emotional needs do not go overlooked.

Finally, adjusting boundaries as needed allows for personal growth and relationship enhancement over time. As people evolve, so too should their boundaries. A boundary that served you well at one point may no longer be necessary, or you might discover a new boundary required as roles and responsibilities change. Being flexible with boundaries does not imply compromising your core values; instead, it highlights adaptability and openness to change.

For example, consider the evolving dynamic between parents and their adult children. As children grow into autonomy, the old parent-child boundaries based on dependency transform into a relationship of mutual respect and independence. This transition often necessitates renegotiation of boundaries to accommodate new roles while honoring the underlying love and care.

Adjusting boundaries underscores the importance of continuous self-reflection and openness to feedback from trusted peers. Growth comes from the willingness to revise personal boundaries while ensuring that they align with personal values and life goals. This flexibility supports healthier interaction with others, allowing for deeper connections rooted in mutual respect.

Guarding Against Manipulation

In the journey of safeguarding your emotional well-being, understanding and protecting yourself from manipulative behaviors is essential. Manipulation can be subtle, making it crucial to recognize red flags early on. Awareness of these tactics not only helps in identifying them but also empowers you to trust your instincts when something feels amiss.

One common sign of manipulation is the inconsistencies between a person's words and actions. A manipulator might make extravagant promises or claim they will change, only for their behavior to remain unchanged. This cycle fosters confusion and self-doubt, weakening your ability to trust your judgment (NERIS Analytics Limited, 2024). Recognizing such patterns enables you to prevent further emotional harm.

Another red flag is gaslighting, where the manipulator lies about events, denying your reality until you question your own memory and sanity. This tactic erodes self-belief, anchoring you deeper into their control. When you see these warning signs, it's vital to acknowledge them without delay and prepare to respond effectively (Manipulators and Predators Are Everywhere! Discover How to Spot Red Flags and Heal from Manipulation!, 2023).

After recognizing these red flags, responding to manipulative attempts becomes imperative. Confrontation doesn't mean aggression; rather, it's about calmly asserting your boundaries. It's pivotal to maintain your composure, calling out the manipulative behavior as soon as it occurs—provided it's safe to do so. Naming specific manipulation techniques and expressing how they impact you can reclaim your autonomy. By questioning motives, you pave the path for healthier interactions.

Learning and practicing assertiveness can bolster your confrontation skills. Assertiveness means communicating your needs confidently while respecting others. This skill can significantly reduce potential conflicts, allowing you to uphold your well-being with dignity and strength. Remember, setting boundaries isn't selfish—it's an act of self-love and respect.

Building emotional awareness also serves as a powerful defense against manipulation. Understanding your emotions gives you the clarity necessary for reflective responses instead of reactive ones. Manipulators often prey on emotional vulnerability, so having insight into your feelings makes it easier to differentiate genuine relations from toxic ones. As you become more attuned to your emotions, you're less likely to fall into manipulative traps.

Creating a support system becomes your fortress during challenging times. Surrounding yourself with trustworthy individuals provides not just comfort but also practical assistance. These relationships offer validation and help you process experiences, keeping you grounded when manipulative influences attempt to sway your perception. A strong support network bolsters resilience, reminding you that you're not alone in your journey towards healing and growth.

It's important to reach out to family and friends who genuinely care about your well-being. Their perspectives can shed light on situations clouded by your emotional involvement, offering a clearer view of the dynamics at play. Sharing your concerns with them can also open doors to much-needed advice and encouragement, fortifying your resolve to stand firm against manipulation.

If confronting manipulation alone seems daunting, professional guidance can be invaluable. Mental health professionals provide tools and strategies tailored to individual experiences, helping you navigate complex relational dynamics. Therapy offers a safe space to unpack emotions, gain insights, and develop personalized strategies to counter manipulation while fostering emotional resilience.

Remember, everyone is susceptible to manipulation regardless of personality type; it's not a reflection of personal weakness. The key lies in educating oneself about manipulative behaviors and cultivating the strength to resist their influence. Trust in your intuition and abilities; you possess the power to reclaim control over your emotional health.

Cultivating Spiritual Resilience

In navigating the complexities of challenging relationships, building spiritual resilience offers a powerful strategy for sustaining one's emotional and spiritual well-being. Spiritual resilience is not merely a defensive mechanism but a dynamic process that enables individuals to harness inner strength during difficult times. At its core lies the ability to find unwavering strength in faith. Many people turn to their spiritual beliefs as a sanctuary amid turmoil. Faith provides a stable foundation, offering comfort and security when external circumstances become turbulent. Research indicates that spirituality can significantly enhance individuals' capacity to manage hardship and facilitate personal growth (Manning et al., 2019; Howard et al., 2023). By aligning oneself with spiritual values and trusting in a higher power, one gains confidence and hope, fostering a resilient mindset crucial for enduring and overcoming adverse situations.

Regular engagement in spiritual practices such as prayer and meditation further bolsters this resilience. These practices create moments of introspection and connection, allowing individuals to gain clarity and peace even amid chaos. Prayer is often seen as a direct channel for seeking guidance and solace, providing a sense of being heard and supported by a divine presence. Meditation, on the other hand, fosters mindfulness and tranquility, equipping individuals with the mental fortitude required to face relational challenges with grace and composure. By incorporating these practices into daily life, individuals nurture their spiritual health, creating an inner reservoir of calmness and clarity on which to draw during trying circumstances.

Furthermore, community and fellowship play a vital role in enhancing spiritual resilience. Participation in spiritual communities offers individuals a network of support where shared beliefs and experiences unite people. These communities often serve as a haven for mutual encouragement, compassion, and empathy. Members often rally around one another during times of need, whether through acts of kindness, listening ears, or collective prayers. The communal aspect of spirituality reinforces individual resilience, as the bonds formed within these groups offer a sense of belonging and solidarity. As highlighted by participants in various studies, having a supportive spiritual community can significantly aid in navigating adversity by providing a dependable social support system (Manning et al., 2019).

Embracing spiritual growth also necessitates welcoming life's challenges as opportunities for transformation. Viewing adversity through a spiritual lens encourages an openness to vulnerability and change. This perspective sees trials not merely as obstacles but as catalysts for maturity and understanding. By actively engaging with spiritual teachings and reflecting on personal experiences, individuals can deepen their faith and cultivate a richer, more mature spiritual identity. This journey of embracing growth involves letting go of rigid self-defenses and opening up to new insights and revelations. It encourages individuals to confront their fears and limitations, transforming them into stepping stones toward greater spiritual awareness and resilience.

Taking these elements together—faith, spiritual practices, community, and a commitment to growth—spiritual resilience emerges as a multifaceted tool that empowers individuals to sustain themselves through challenging relationships. It is both an internal and communal process, drawing upon personal beliefs and practices while being enriched by the collective support and wisdom of others. Embracing these aspects allows individuals to navigate toxic environments with a fortified spirit, enabling them to maintain their peace and integrity despite external challenges. As research suggests, spirituality functions as a protective factor associated with improved well-being and resilience, guiding individuals through life's adversities (Howard et al., 2023).

Summary and Reflections

Throughout this chapter, we've explored essential strategies to protect your emotional and spiritual well-being. By identifying and setting personal boundaries, you learn the importance of self-awareness and clear communication in nurturing healthier relationships. These boundaries, coupled with assertive communication, help you effectively manage interactions and preserve your peace of mind. Reflecting on relationship dynamics allows you to recognize which connections truly support your growth and where adjustments might be necessary.

As we also guard against manipulation, recognizing red flags becomes vital to maintaining mental resilience. Learning to confront these behaviors with calm confidence can safeguard your autonomy. Building a solid support network further fortifies your emotional defenses, providing the validation and guidance needed along your journey. By incorporating spiritual practices and embracing community support, you gain strength and clarity, equipping you to face challenges with hope and faith. Remember, nurturing your spirit and emotions is an ongoing process—a path towards healing and a future filled with promise.

Chapter Six
Understanding the Manipulation

Understanding the manipulation within a toxic relationship is essential for those seeking clarity and healing. By shedding light on behaviors that often go unnoticed, individuals can begin to untangle the web of control and regain their sense of self. For many, these relationships start subtly, with small actions or words that seem insignificant at first. As time goes on, however, these manipulations compound, leaving one feeling lost and unsure of their own identity. Recognizing these patterns is a brave and crucial step in breaking free from the cycle of emotional turmoil that manipulators create.

This chapter delves into the various tactics employed in toxic relationships to control and manipulate. Readers will explore how micro-aggressions slowly chip away at an individual's self-worth and how withdrawal of communication can be used as a form of punishment. Love bombing, a deceptive tactic wrapped in affection, will also be examined for its role in creating dependency. Furthermore, readers will gain insights into the psychological effects of these manipulations, including anxiety and low self-esteem. Through this exploration, the chapter aims to equip individuals with the knowledge needed to recognize and address manipulation, fostering a journey toward personal empowerment and healing.

Recognizing Subtle Manipulation

Navigating the complexities of toxic relationships requires an understanding of the subtle and often overlooked tactics used by manipulators. One such tactic is micro-aggressions, which are minor yet insidious behaviors employed to undermine a partner's self-esteem. These can manifest as offhand comments or dismissive actions that make an individual doubt their own worth, shaking the foundations of their identity. For instance, seemingly casual remarks about one's appearance or abilities may gradually accumulate, eroding confidence over time. As self-doubt grows, it becomes easier for manipulators to exert control, leading individuals to feel more reliant on their partners' approval.

Another common but harmful tactic is the silent treatment. Unlike overt aggression, this method involves withdrawing communication as a form of punishment or control. The impact of this can be profound, causing emotional distress and insecurity in the victim. When communication lines are cut, the recipient often experiences anxiety and confusion, unsure how to reconcile the situation or mend the rift. This not only places power firmly in the manipulator's hands but also keeps the victim in a state of emotional turmoil, continually seeking reconciliation and validation from their partner.

Love bombing presents a particularly deceptive front, cloaked in affection and attention that initially appears heartwarming. This overwhelming display of love—replete with grand gestures, constant communication, and intense companionship—can obscure the underlying manipulative intent. Initially, victims may feel cherished and valued, but as the relationship progresses, it becomes evident that this barrage of affection is less about genuine love and more about creating dependency. The roller coaster effect of high-intensity affection followed by withdrawal serves to confuse and bind the victim emotionally, blurring the line between genuine care and control (Stritof, 2023).

In many cases, manipulators adeptly use the tactic of playing the victim. By casting themselves as misunderstood or unfairly treated, they shift focus away from their own behavior and onto how others have wronged them. This strategy effectively garners sympathy and aids in evading responsibility for their actions. Consequently, the true victim is often left questioning their perception of events and may even feel compelled to comfort and support the manipulator, despite being the one harmed. Perpetrators skillfully weave narratives that paint them in a pitiable light, making it challenging for outsiders—and even the victim—to recognize the manipulation at play (*What Are Ghosting, Benching, Gaslighting, and Lovebombing? Tactics of Emotional Abuse. - Becky's Fund*, 2017).

Psychological Effects of Control

In toxic relationships, manipulation and coercive control can create an environment of uncertainty that significantly affects mental health. Imagine living in a world where the ground beneath you constantly shifts, never knowing what tomorrow might hold. This unpredictability is a hallmark of manipulative dynamics, often leading to anxiety disorders. When someone is subjected to erratic behavior or inconsistent communication, it becomes impossible to find stability or peace of mind. The constant state of alertness takes a toll on one's emotional well-being, making anxiety a natural response to the chaos instigated by manipulation.

Furthermore, the repetitive cycle of manipulation gradually erodes self-esteem. It's akin to water wearing away stone; initially imperceptible, but eventually undeniable. In these interactions, individuals are systematically made to question their worth and identity. They become convinced of their inadequacy, as manipulators purposely diminish their achievements and belittle their capabilities. Over time, this relentless assault on one's self-concept leads to feelings of worthlessness and diminished confidence. However, recognizing this link between low self-esteem and manipulation can motivate those affected to embark on a journey of personal healing and rediscovery (Güler et al., 2022).

Cognitive dissonance, another psychological phenomenon, arises when there's a disconnect between what one perceives and the narrative pushed by the manipulator. Victims find themselves trapped in a web of conflicting thoughts and beliefs. They grapple with balancing their own perceptions against the twisted reality presented to them. This internal struggle can be exhausting, as the individual endeavors to resolve these contradictory beliefs. Identifying cognitive dissonance is crucial for untangling these complex emotions and regaining a sense of clarity.

Isolation is a powerful tool frequently employed by manipulators to reinforce their control. By cutting victims off from their support networks, they effectively increase dependency on the abuser. Friends, family, and even colleagues may be deliberately alienated, leaving the victim without the necessary perspective to see the relationship's toxicity. This isolation not only deprives individuals of external validation that could challenge the manipulator's narrative, but it also amplifies feelings of loneliness and helplessness. Understanding this tactic helps victims recognize the importance of re-establishing connections with supportive people who can provide encouragement and strength.

Navigating the detrimental effects of manipulation requires a concerted effort toward recovery. Acknowledging the presence of anxiety, low self-esteem, cognitive dissonance, and isolation is an essential first step. Seeking professional guidance through therapy or counseling can help uncover the roots of these issues, empowering individuals to rewrite their narratives and reclaim their lives. Building a circle of trusted friends and family, albeit difficult, offers a foundation of love and reassurance. Each interaction with this network serves as a reminder of one's inherent value and capacity for growth, counteracting the manipulative tactics' damaging impact.

Biblical Stories of Manipulation

In exploring the biblical tales that illustrate manipulation, Jacob's story presents a profound lesson about deceit and its consequences. The account of Jacob and Esau shines a light on how manipulating situations can lead to lasting repercussions. In Genesis 27, Jacob deceives his father Isaac into giving him the blessing meant for his brother Esau. While Jacob gains what he desires in the short term, this act of deceit causes a rift between the brothers, leading Jacob to flee for his life. This separation marks a journey of hardship and self-discovery for Jacob, where he encounters further deception himself, such as Laban's ploy discussed later. From this narrative, we learn that deceitful actions can ripple through one's life, creating unexpected challenges and shaping one's journey towards integrity and reconciliation.

Moving to the tale of Delilah and Samson, found in Judges 16, we delve into the destructive force of betrayal through manipulation. Delilah uses emotional tactics to unravel Samson's secrets, ultimately leading to his downfall. Her persistence in questioning, combined with affectionate gestures, wears down Samson's resolve. Once she learns that his strength lies in his uncut hair, she betrays him, resulting in his capture by the Philistines. Samson's vulnerability to

Delilah's manipulation serves as a stark reminder of how emotional exploitation can have devastating effects. The loss of his strength signifies not just a physical defeat but also a spiritual decline, highlighting the importance of guarding oneself against deceptive influences that prey on vulnerabilities.

Jezebel's story in 1 Kings 21 exemplifies manipulation wielded for power and control. By orchestrating the unjust execution of Naboth to seize his vineyard, Jezebel showcases the dark potential of deceit used in the pursuit of authority. Her ability to manipulate King Ahab and the elders reflects a profound warning: when manipulation is driven by ambition, it leads to destructive outcomes not only for the victims but also for those who partake in deceitful schemes. Jezebel's deception results in dire consequences for her and her family, emphasizing a biblical truth about the perils of pursuing power through unrighteous means. Her story warns us of the moral decay and chaos that ensue when manipulation becomes a tool for personal gain.

The narrative of Potiphar's wife offers another angle on manipulation's impact, illustrating the dangers of false accusations and their repercussions. In Genesis 39, Joseph, a man of integrity, finds himself wrongfully accused of making advances toward Potiphar's wife after repeatedly rejecting her attempts to seduce him. Her manipulative lie lands Joseph in prison, underscoring how deceitful actions can alter someone's life trajectory. Yet, Joseph's steadfastness in maintaining his integrity amidst adversity speaks volumes about the power of character in the face of manipulation. His eventual rise to prominence in Egypt serves as a testament to the enduring strength of honesty and the belief that truth ultimately prevails over deceit.

Understanding these biblical narratives equips us with valuable lessons for recognizing and navigating manipulation in relationships today. These stories underscore the complexities of human interactions where trust can be exploited, and power can corrupt. By reflecting on these teachings, we can discern the subtle signs of deceit and empower ourselves to uphold integrity and authenticity. For individuals feeling trapped in toxic relationships, these ancient tales offer timeless wisdom on the importance of staying true to one's core values even when faced with manipulation.

For Christian counselors and support group leaders, these biblical examples provide rich material for fostering discussions about the moral and spiritual dimensions of manipulation. They serve as a foundation for guiding others toward healing by highlighting the virtues of forgiveness, resilience, and discernment. Integrating these stories into counseling sessions can encourage individuals to recognize manipulation patterns and develop strategies to protect their mental and emotional well-being.

To deal with manipulation, recognizing gaslighting becomes crucial. Gaslighting is a psychological tactic where manipulators distort reality to make their victims doubt themselves or question their sanity. Recognizing these red flags early can promote proactive responses to controlling dynamics. Some signs include persistent lying, contradicting previous statements, invalidating feelings, and isolating the victim from support systems. When aware of these patterns, individuals can build resilience and seek help, thus counteracting the manipulator's influence.

Final Insights

In this chapter, we've explored the nuanced tactics used in toxic relationships to manipulate and control. From the erosion of self-esteem through micro-aggressions to the emotional turmoil inflicted by silent treatments, these subtle yet harmful behaviors are designed to destabilize and confuse. Love bombing can seem like a genuine expression of affection but ultimately chains individuals emotionally, creating dependency. The manipulator's ability to play the victim often shifts blame and obscures their role in causing harm, leaving others questioning reality. These behaviors are interwoven with psychological effects such as anxiety and cognitive dissonance, which further entrench control over victims. Recognizing these patterns is essential for breaking free from their grasp and beginning the journey toward healing.

Drawing lessons from biblical stories, we gain insight into the timeless struggle against manipulation. Whether it's Jacob's deceit, Samson's betrayal, or Jezebel's power-driven schemes, these narratives remind us of the consequences manipulation can bring. They offer hope that despite deceit and control, integrity and truth have the power to prevail. For those feeling trapped in such relationships, reflection on these stories provides encouragement to stay true to one's values and seek support from trusted networks. Christian counselors and support group leaders can use these teachings to guide conversations about morality and resilience, equipping individuals with the understanding and faith needed to overcome manipulative influences.

Chapter Seven
Balancing Boundaries with Grace

Balancing boundaries with grace is essential in managing relationships that might otherwise feel overwhelming or toxic. Establishing firm boundaries helps protect one's mental and emotional health, ensuring individuals do not fall prey to manipulation or neglect their well-being. However, balancing these boundaries with grace requires more than just drawing lines; it involves integrating compassion and understanding into interactions, fostering healthier connections. The delicate act of setting these boundaries calls for a blend of firmness and empathy, emphasizing the need to remain true to oneself while extending kindness to others. With patience and thoughtful reflection, establishing such boundaries becomes an empowering act of self-care rather than selfishness, paving the way for more genuine and fulfilling relationships.

This chapter delves into various techniques for effective boundary setting, providing practical advice on how to communicate needs clearly and assertively without aggression. Readers will explore ways to handle resistance gracefully, understanding that pushback often comes from others' insecurities rather than their own faults. Additionally, the chapter emphasizes the importance of regular evaluation and adjustment of boundaries to align with personal growth and changing life circumstances. Through relatable narratives and insights, it guides readers on how to weave patience and understanding into their boundary-setting practices, ultimately transforming these experiences into opportunities for deeper connections. By learning to navigate this balance, readers are encouraged to uphold their dignity and respect, allowing room for both personal development and healthier relationships with those around them.

Techniques for Effective Boundary Setting

Establishing firm boundaries while embodying grace is a delicate balance, vital for emotional health and well-being. Recognizing personal limits is the first step toward preventing manipulation and avoiding overwhelm. When we acknowledge our own capacities, we become more aware of situations that could lead to discomfort or distress if not managed with care. Understanding these boundaries helps us discern when someone is overstepping or when we are stretching ourselves too thin at the expense of our mental and emotional state. By identifying these personal limits, individuals can take proactive measures to shield themselves from negative influences that harm their peace.

Communicating boundaries assertively is equally important. It is essential to express your needs and expectations clearly to ensure mutual respect and understanding. Assertive communication doesn't mean being aggressive; rather, it involves speaking your truth calmly and confidently, without belittling others. This approach fosters an environment of open dialogue and cooperation, reducing potential conflicts and misunderstandings. Clear articulation of boundaries sets a standard for acceptable behavior, guiding those around you to respect your space and emotions. Practice stating your needs directly and positively, focusing on what you want instead of what you don't want (Nash, 2018).

In anticipation of resistance, it's crucial to understand that pushback often reflects the other person's issues rather than your fault. It's common for some individuals to challenge established boundaries as they may feel threatened by change or fear losing control. Recognizing this tendency allows you to remain grounded and composed when faced with opposition.

Resistance doesn't necessarily mean that you're in the wrong; it simply highlights the areas that need careful navigation and potential reassurance. Stand firm in your convictions and maintain dignity and respect, allowing room for the other person's perspective while also holding steady to your established limits. Be prepared for this resistance by understanding the psychological aspects of boundary challenges and maintaining a compassionate yet firm stance.

Regular evaluation and adjustment of boundaries keep them relevant and supportive of growth. Just as life circumstances evolve, so too should your boundaries. What worked in one phase of life might not be applicable in another. Through regular self-reflection, you can assess whether your boundaries continue to serve your emotional health and align with your values. If you find that certain limits are no longer effective, don't hesitate to modify them to better fit your current situation. This continuous adaptation ensures that your boundaries remain constructive and compatible with your evolving self. It requires introspection and sometimes difficult conversations but ultimately leads to improved relationships and a stronger sense of self.

To effectively establish these boundaries while practicing grace, one must weave patience and understanding into the process. Rather than perceiving boundaries as rigid walls, view them as flexible guidelines that foster healthy interaction and mutual respect. Encourage others to share their perspectives and actively listen to their concerns, which promotes empathy and connection. This approach does not imply compromising your boundaries but rather integrating compassion into your interactions. Allow room for learning and growth on both sides, which can transform boundary-setting experiences into opportunities for enhanced understanding and deeper relationships.

Practice assertiveness, not as a tool for confrontation but as a means to express authenticity and affirm your worth, reinforcing the importance of maintaining respectful interactions (*How to Defend Your Boundaries and Be Assertive*, 2023). Embrace the discomfort that may arise from establishing boundaries as a natural part of the process. Guilt or reluctance is normal, especially if raised in environments where prioritizing self was seen as selfish or wrong. However, acknowledging these feelings and moving through them is integral to building healthier, more balanced relationships. Remember that setting boundaries is an act of self-care, not selfishness, paving the way for more genuine and fulfilling connections.

Role of Forgiveness in Healing

Forgiveness is an essential part of healing, even when boundaries need to be maintained. Understanding that forgiveness doesn't necessarily mean reconciliation provides a vital safeguard against falling back into toxic relationships. Often, people equate forgiving someone with mending the relationship fully, but forgiveness involves releasing oneself from the burden of resentment without re-entering unhealthy dynamics. This principle is especially important in situations where rebuilding a relationship might not be safe or beneficial.

The act of forgiveness itself can be a profound release. Holding onto anger or bitterness toward someone who has hurt you consumes emotional energy and mental space, diverting it away from personal growth and well-being. By letting go of the negative emotions associated with past hurts, individuals can redirect their focus on more productive and fulfilling pursuits. Letting go of these burdens allows for a clearer vision of one's path forward, promoting overall health and happiness.

Scripture provides a wealth of wisdom on how to approach forgiveness. Biblical teachings emphasize the importance of forgiving others as God forgives us, highlighting this process as a pathway to peace and inner harmony. For example, Colossians 3:13 advises believers to forgive grievances as the Lord forgives, reminding us that forgiveness is both a spiritual command and a tool for personal serenity (Buckles, 2024). Rather than viewing forgiveness as merely a moral obligation, interpreting it as a divine guide offers deeper significance and clarity.

Moreover, biblical narratives offer numerous examples of forgiveness in action. Stories like that of Joseph and his brothers illustrate how forgiving severe wrongs can lead to redemption and transformation, even though reconciliation may or may not follow. These stories provide comfort and direction, showing that forgiveness is possible and beneficial even in complex circumstances.

Practicing forgiveness daily encourages a lasting emotional release, fostering a change that goes beyond temporary relief. It's one thing to forgive a single incident on a single day; it's another to integrate forgiveness into one's lifestyle. Making a habit of forgiveness enriches our lives by progressively lightening emotional loads we carry. It becomes easier to maintain a state of grace and less taxing to navigate interpersonal conflicts, which often arise unexpectedly.

To embed forgiveness into daily life, individuals can start by cultivating mindfulness and self-awareness. Recognizing emotional triggers and observing reactions helps in understanding when to initiate the forgiveness process. Pausing to assess feelings before they escalate into resentment allows individuals to consider healthier responses. Over time, developing this awareness shapes how we interact not only with those who hurt us but also with ourselves.

Incorporating prayer and meditation into daily routines reinforces this practice. These activities create spaces for reflection and connection with spiritual beliefs, supporting the ongoing journey of forgiveness. Engaging with such practices can reassure individuals they are never alone in their struggles, providing strength and encouragement when faced with difficult relationships.

Consistency in practicing forgiveness requires patience, discipline, and sometimes guidance from others. This consistency nurtures emotional resilience, helping individuals recover more swiftly from emotional upheavals. It is particularly helpful to have a faith community or support network that shares similar values. They can offer empathy and perspective, reinforcing commitment to the path of forgiveness when wavering seems tempting.

A supportive community can also remind individuals of scriptural teachings and practical advice on maintaining peace and well-being. Counselors or group leaders within these communities play a key role by facilitating discussions on forgiveness and boundaries.

As guides, they help others navigate the complexities of toxic relationships, encouraging forgiveness without sacrificing personal safety and dignity.

Ultimately, respecting one's own boundaries while pursuing forgiveness allows people to remain open-hearted yet protected. It's about finding equilibrium—extending grace to oneself as much as to others. Remembering that forgiveness doesn't obligate us to stay in harmful situations aligns with the biblical call to protect our hearts and minds.

Maintaining Grace Under Pressure

In moments when our boundaries are tested, maintaining grace and composure becomes crucial. For many of us navigating toxic relationships, or guiding others through them, this can be a delicate balance. It requires patience, thoughtful reflection, compassion, and support systems that nourish our emotional well-being.

Patience, often an undervalued virtue, plays a pivotal role in handling challenging situations. When our boundaries are pushed or disregarded, the instinct might be to react immediately and defensively. However, such reactions can often escalate conflicts rather than resolve them. By practicing patience, we allow ourselves time to assess the situation calmly and make clear, sound decisions. According to Winston Churchill's timeless advice to "keep calm and carry on," staying composed not only helps in managing emotional distress but also supports clearer thinking (ComplexityBeauty, 2024). Keeping calm prevents emotional turbulence from clouding our judgment and allows us to approach challenges with a level-headed perspective.

Furthermore, reflecting before reacting is integral to maintaining grace under pressure. In her research, Tasha Eurich highlights the importance of self-awareness and its impact on decision-making and effective communication (Harvard Professional Development, 2019). Taking a moment to pause, breathe, and reflect before responding to provocation helps ensure that our actions align with our core values and principles. This mindful approach prevents impulsive reactions, which often exacerbate tensions, allowing us instead to offer thoughtful responses. Such responses are more likely to facilitate understanding and resolution, reinforcing the boundaries we have set without aggression or resentment.

While patience and reflection are tools for prevention, embracing compassion during conflict helps shift the dynamics from confrontation to understanding.

Compassion doesn't mean accepting mistreatment or compromising personal boundaries; rather, it involves shifting the focus from hostility to empathy. By trying to understand the emotions and perspectives of those testing our boundaries, we might find common ground or uncover underlying issues contributing to their behavior. This empathetic engagement promotes a gentler dialogue and fosters a sense of mutual respect, decreasing the likelihood of further conflict.

Another powerful strategy when maintaining composure in difficult moments is to utilize support systems. During periods of stress, leaning on trusted friends, family, or support groups provides not just emotional grounding but also practical advice and encouragement. Organizational psychologist Andrews notes that those who practice self-regulation often rely on their network to manage stressful situations effectively (Harvard Professional Development, 2019). Trusted advisors can offer fresh perspectives, helping you navigate boundary-challenging situations with poise and strength. They can also remind you of your inherent value and the validity of your boundaries, offering reassurance when self-doubt creeps in.

For individuals who feel trapped in toxic relationships, community and spiritual support can be invaluable. Engaging with others who share similar experiences provides comfort and solidarity. Sharing insights and strategies for coping enhances collective resilience, making the journey less daunting. Moreover, finding solace in spiritual practices or teachings can help reinforce the inner peace and fortitude necessary to maintain grace while upholding boundaries. Biblical teachings, for instance, offer guidance on patience, forgiveness, and empathy, empowering individuals to handle adversity with faith and integrity.

Lastly, it's important to acknowledge that the journey toward maintaining composure in the face of boundary challenges is ongoing. Emotional intelligence isn't static; it's developed over time with conscious effort and practice. Setting realistic expectations for oneself and celebrating small victories along the way can bolster confidence and encourage continued growth. Every step taken, whether big or small, is a testament to one's strength and commitment to healthier, more respectful interactions.

To conclude, cultivating patience, practicing reflection, embracing compassion, and drawing on supportive networks form a robust framework for gracefully managing boundary tests. These strategies not only safeguard our emotional well-being but also promote healthier, more balanced relationships. As we strive to uphold boundaries with grace, let us remember that each experience is an opportunity to grow stronger and wiser, equipping us to face future challenges with increased resilience and peace.

Final Thoughts

In this chapter, we delved into the art of setting firm boundaries while maintaining forgiveness as a cornerstone of emotional well-being. Boundaries serve as essential guidelines that protect us from negative influences and guide others in respecting our space. By asserting these limits clearly and with compassion, we create an environment where mutual respect thrives. We explored how boundary setting is not about building walls but rather about fostering healthy interactions that prioritize personal peace and dignity. Recognizing and adjusting our boundaries according to life's changes ensures they remain supportive, helping us grow stronger and more resilient over time. This dynamic approach to boundaries allows us not only to safeguard our well-being but also to build more honest and fulfilling connections.

Equally important is the role of forgiveness in healing from past hurts, liberating us from resentment's heavy burden. Forgiveness does not always mean reconciliation but rather a release that enables personal growth. Through biblical teachings, we are reminded that forgiving others mirrors divine grace, leading to inner peace and harmony. Embracing forgiveness fosters emotional resilience and encourages a lifestyle where empathy prevails over conflict. In moments when boundaries are tested, patience and reflection become key, enabling thoughtful responses rather than impulsive reactions. By utilizing support systems and leaning on spiritual guidance, we can navigate challenges gracefully, upholding both our boundaries and our compassion for others. Balancing these elements ultimately empowers us to handle adversity with strength, nurturing healthier relationships grounded in respect and understanding.

Chapter Eight
Tools for Personal Growth

Personal growth requires tools and strategies that help individuals navigate the complex terrain of self-discovery, particularly following the end of a significant relationship. In this chapter, we delve into the practical steps one can take to not only cope with the aftermath but also to foster a journey of profound personal development. When relationships conclude, especially tumultuous ones, there is often an opportunity—or perhaps necessity—to reflect deeply on one's life, values, and goals. This period of introspection offers a fertile ground for transformation, urging individuals to explore their inner selves with curiosity and compassion. The process involves shedding old layers and embracing new perspectives, ideally leading to a sense of renewal and empowerment.

Within these pages, readers will uncover various methods designed to facilitate this transformative journey. We start by exploring the cathartic practice of journaling—a gateway to emotional clarity and self-awareness. By documenting thoughts and feelings without judgment, individuals begin to unravel emotional complexities, creating space for healing and growth. The chapter further investigates the role of affirmations in reshaping self-perception, serving as powerful antidotes to negative internal dialogues. Alongside, the significance of setting clear, value-aligned goals emerges as a cornerstone of progress, emphasizing actionable steps toward envisioned futures. Moreover, we discuss how identifying behavioral patterns through reflective writing can guide informed decision-making, allowing readers to recognize and adjust habits that either hinder or enhance their personal journey. Through these explorations, the chapter aims to equip both individuals seeking solace and counselors guiding others with valuable insights and actionable strategies, fostering a supportive environment for sustainable personal growth.

Journaling for Self-Discovery

In moments of reflection, journaling emerges as a powerful tool for personal growth and emotional clarity, particularly following the turmoil of leaving a toxic relationship. This practice is more than simply putting pen to paper; it serves as a means to navigate complicated emotions, enhance self-awareness, and ultimately, guide the journey of healing.

Journaling offers a safe space where feelings and thoughts can be expressed freely, unearthing layers of emotional burdens that might otherwise remain unspoken. When individuals write without judgment, they allow themselves to embrace vulnerability, an essential step towards emotional release. This process can alleviate the weight of unresolved feelings, replacing chaos with clarity and fostering a deeper understanding of one's emotional landscape (University of Rochester Medical Center, 2019). In doing so, journaling acts as a mirror, reflecting back not only immediate emotions but also underlying triggers and patterns.

Amidst the continuous journey of personal development, documenting one's daily experiences in a journal becomes a critical exercise in recognizing behavioral patterns. Through consistent entries, individuals often uncover recurring themes or responses to specific situations. These insights serve as a valuable resource for informed decision-making, allowing individuals to identify behaviors that hinder progress or promote positive change. By objectively analyzing their entries, they craft a narrative that highlights growth areas and potential obstacles, setting the stage for intentional change (WebMD.com, 2021).

Moreover, incorporating affirmations into journaling is an empowering technique to combat negative self-talk

—an all-too-common residue of destructive relationships. Positive affirmations written consistently in a journal are not mere words; they are declarations of self-worth and strength. These affirmations help reshape mental narratives by focusing on personal capabilities and achievements rather than failures or inadequacies (Sohal et al., 2022). They act as steadfast reminders of resilience and inner power, gradually shifting the mindset from self-doubt to self-assurance.

Setting goals and aspirations within the pages of a journal can initiate a roadmap for recovery and growth. By outlining clear objectives, individuals create a forward-looking vision that adds purpose to their healing journey. Structured plans encourage prioritization of steps necessary for personal development, acting as benchmarks against which progress is measured. The act of writing these goals down reinforces self-efficacy, as individuals witness their own commitment to change and personal empowerment through documented milestones (Fredrickson, 2010).

For many undergoing the transformative process of post-relationship healing, journaling becomes a lifeline, connecting them to their innermost selves. This practice bridges the gap between past trauma and future aspirations, ultimately guiding them toward a renewed sense of identity. While engaging in regular journaling, practitioners experience not only emotional catharsis but also cognitive processing as they weave coherence from their narratives. It's a journey that encourages mindful acceptance of their unique emotional truths, aligning actions with newfound understandings of self (Forsyth & Eifert, 2016).

As journeys of healing unfold, the practical benefits of journaling cannot be overstated. It's important for individuals to incorporate guidelines that enhance the effectiveness of this practice. Firstly, identifying patterns in journal entries helps recognize recurring emotional or situational trends that impact well-being. This insight assists in developing strategies to either address adverse patterns or reinforce positive ones. Secondly, setting affirmations during journaling acts as an antidote to the internalized criticisms left behind by toxic relationships, paving the way for healthier self-perception.

Finally, creating a roadmap for personal development within journals infuses purpose into the healing process. Individuals benefit from clearly defined goals that transform abstract desires into actionable steps. Journals thus become ongoing projects of self-improvement, tracking achievements and recalibrating paths as needed, which reinforces confidence and fosters continuous growth.

Setting New Personal Goals

Recovering from a relationship often marks a crucial turning point in one's personal journey. It's a moment ripe for self-reflection and growth, where setting new, healthy goals can become a powerful antidote to the emotional turmoil of the past. These goals, when aligned with personal values, can foster a renewed sense of purpose and direction.

Utilizing the SMART Goals Framework serves as an effective method in this process because it promotes clarity and focus, two essential elements when attempting to navigate the foggy aftermath of a challenging relationship. The SMART acronym stands for Specific, Measurable, Achievable, Relevant, and Time-bound. By committing to this structured goal-setting approach, individuals can create a roadmap that not only guides them toward their aspirations but also significantly reduces overwhelming feelings one might encounter during the recovery phase. For instance, rather than vaguely deciding to "get healthier," a specific goal using the SMART framework might be, "I will attend a yoga class every Tuesday and Thursday evening for the next three months." This clear articulation provides measurable steps and a time frame, ensuring the goal is both realistic and relevant to immediate needs (Alberts, 2024).

Equally important is aligning your objectives with core personal values. When goals resonate with what truly matters in life, they become more than just targets to hit; they evolve into meaningful pursuits that fulfill a deeper sense of self-worth. For example, if compassion is a core value, setting a goal to volunteer regularly at a local shelter can yield profound personal satisfaction and motivation. This alignment not only fosters intrinsic motivation but also establishes a strong foundation for future decision-making, supporting actions that honor one's sense of integrity and worthiness.

Building accountability systems further enhances commitment by incorporating external support. Regular check-ins with trusted friends, mentors, or even a counselor can serve as an anchor, offering encouragement and constructive feedback. These interactions help track progress and make any necessary adjustments to the plan. An accountability partner could be someone who shares similar goals or simply someone you trust to provide honest reflections on your journey. They can act as a mirror, reflecting on your achievements and setbacks and helping maintain focus and momentum. Engaging with supportive communities, whether through organized groups or informal networks, amplifies these efforts by fostering a shared environment of growth and mutual encouragement. Accountability not only provides external validation but also instills a sense of responsibility towards those who've invested in your progress. Regular updates and discussions with an accountability partner strengthen resolve, ensuring you remain dedicated to the path you've chosen (5 Psychology-Backed Tips to Stay Committed to Your New Year Goals - Mindstate Psychology Blog, 2024).

Celebrating small victories is another key element in maintaining motivation and reinforcing positive changes along this transformative journey. Each achievement, no matter how minor, contributes to a larger picture of personal development and resilience. Recognizing these milestones can bolster confidence and remind you of the progress made, serving as tangible evidence of ongoing commitment to self-improvement. Whether it's successfully sticking to a weekly exercise routine or completing a course that boosts career prospects, these moments deserve acknowledgment and celebration. They are not just checkpoints; they are affirmations of your ability to overcome obstacles and adapt to change. Celebrating achievements reinforces positive habits and provides psychological rewards, making the pursuit of larger goals feel less daunting and more achievable.

In crafting new goals post-relationship, it is also vital to acknowledge the social and environmental factors that can influence success. Surroundings and interpersonal dynamics play pivotal roles in shaping behavior and steering change. Creating an environment conducive to growth may mean eliminating triggers or distractions that hinder progress while cultivating spaces and relationships that inspire and support desired behaviors. This intentional curation of one's milieu involves being mindful of influences—positive or negative—that impact the journey towards self-betterment. It's about choosing companions who uplift rather than drain energy and designing physical spaces that promote rather than stifle productivity. Through this awareness, individuals can build habitats that nurture aspirations and reflect the evolving self, enhancing the likelihood of sustained personal development.

Embracing Community Support

In the journey of personal growth after emerging from a challenging relationship, finding and embracing supportive communities play a critical role in healing and development. These networks provide not only validation but also a sense of belonging, which is essential for emotional recuperation. Engaging with others who have faced similar experiences allows individuals to feel understood and valued, reducing feelings of isolation.

Finding support networks is foundational for anyone seeking healing. Joining groups or communities centered around personal development can be an excellent start. These spaces serve as safe havens where people can share their stories, listen to others, and collectively explore beneficial coping strategies. For instance, attending support group meetings or participating in online forums dedicated to personal growth encourages open dialogue and mutual understanding. These environments offer more than just comfort; they present opportunities to learn and apply practical techniques that aid in overcoming emotional hurdles. Networks like these enable members to access diverse resources such as workshops, seminars, and counseling services, further strengthening their resolve and resilience.

A guideline worth considering when engaging with support networks is to choose communities that resonate with one's values and goals. It's important to seek out spaces where genuine connections can be formed and maintained. These networks should offer opportunities for meaningful interaction, whether through regular meetings, social events, or collaborative projects. A community that aligns with personal beliefs not only strengthens your support system but also enriches your development journey by providing relevant insights and fostering long-lasting relationships.

Building healthy relationships within these communities is another crucial aspect of personal growth. Positive influences cultivated through these connections can significantly impact one's life journey by modeling supportive and nurturing dynamics. Having mentors or peers who inspire confidence and hold you accountable can reinforce self-assurance, helping you stay true to your path of recovery. By observing how others navigate challenges and maintain positivity, individuals can adopt similar practices in their own lives.

Healthy relationships often involve mutual respect, clear communication, and consistent support. It's about surrounding oneself with those who understand the importance of boundaries and reciprocity, ensuring that each individual feels valued and heard. Cultivating such relationships requires intention and effort, but the rewards are profound, as they foster an environment where one feels empowered to grow and thrive.

For many, engaging in faith communities is another avenue for personal and spiritual growth. These communities provide a unique form of support that nurtures the soul and spirit. Being part of a faith-based group offers a sense of peace and hope, often rooted in shared beliefs and practices. Services, prayer groups, or faith-based gatherings allow individuals to connect on a deeper level, offering solace and encouragement during tough times. The spiritual guidance found here reinforces a sense of purpose and belonging, aiding in emotional healing and fostering inner peace.

Within these faith communities, members often find comfort in rituals and traditions that provide structure and meaning. Participating in communal activities, volunteering within the congregation, or simply being an active member can deepen one's connection to their faith and fellow believers. This shared spiritual journey enhances personal growth, offering new perspectives on life's challenges and inspiring a renewed sense of hope and optimism.

Volunteering and service are powerful tools for shifting focus from personal pain to collective support. Engaging in acts of service not only benefits the community but also aids in personal healing by developing empathy and expanding perspectives. Volunteering provides a sense of purpose and fulfillment, reminding individuals of their ability to make a positive impact despite past adversities.

Through volunteering, individuals learn to prioritize the needs of others, which can be both humbling and uplifting. It broadens one's understanding of diverse situations and challenges, encouraging a more compassionate outlook on life. By giving back, volunteers often discover newfound joys and strengths, contributing to their overall personal growth and stability.

Concluding Thoughts

Navigating life after a challenging relationship can feel like wandering through a dense fog, but the right tools and support can illuminate the path to healing. This chapter explored how vital personal development is during such transformative times, with journaling emerging as a particularly powerful method for self-discovery and growth. Through the act of writing, individuals uncover hidden emotions and patterns that may have entrenched them in negativity. Journaling offers not only a release but also clarity about what truly matters, setting a solid foundation for positive change. Pairing this personal reflection with goal-setting strategies like the SMART framework can further solidify one's journey forward, creating achievable milestones that reinforce a renewed sense of purpose.

Moreover, embracing community support provides additional strength in this journey. Healing is often amplified by sharing experiences within supportive networks where emotional wounds find validation and understanding. These connections offer encouragement, reduce isolation, and foster resilience, transforming pain into collective empowerment. Engaging with groups that share similar values builds an environment conducive to growth, helping individuals reclaim their identity and sense of worth. Whether through faith communities or volunteer opportunities, these interactions cultivate empathy and hope. Together, journaling, goal-setting, and community support form a triad of healing, guiding individuals toward a future filled with possibilities and peace.

Chapter Nine
Stories of Triumph

Triumphing over adversity is a journey marked by courage, resilience, and profound personal transformation. In times when toxic relationships threaten to erode one's sense of self-worth and autonomy, finding the strength to break free becomes an act of both survival and renewal. The path to liberation from these harmful dynamics often involves confronting deep-seated fears, navigating complex emotions, and forging a new identity built on self-discovery and empowerment. The stories that emerge from these journeys of triumph offer invaluable insights into the raw and transformative power of reclaiming one's life, illustrating that even in the darkest moments, hope and healing are attainable. As individuals embark on this challenging yet rewarding path, they craft narratives that not only spotlight their resilience but also inspire others facing similar battles to believe in their potential for change.

Within this chapter, readers will delve into compelling testimonies of individuals who have overcome the shadows of toxic relationships. Each story paints a vivid picture of personal growth and recovery while highlighting the diverse strategies and support systems that aid in the journey towards empowerment. Through experiences shared by Lisa, William, Maria, and John, this chapter explores various facets of healing—ranging from emotional independence and the power of community to the pivotal role of spirituality and self-love. The lessons gleaned from these narratives serve as guiding lights, fostering a deeper understanding of the steps necessary to rebuild lives entrenched in positivity and hope. By examining these tales of victory, the chapter aims to provide readers with not only a sense of solidarity but also practical insights and encouragement to follow their own paths toward liberation and fulfillment.

Transformative Personal Stories

Lisa's journey out of a controlling relationship demonstrates the profound strength necessary to break free from toxicity. Initially trapped in a cycle of fear and manipulation, Lisa began to recognize the toll it was taking on her emotional well-being. Despite the challenges she faced, including financial dependence and the isolation imposed by her partner, Lisa gathered the courage to seek help. With the support of friends and a local women's group, she devised a plan to leave safely. This transition was not just about physical separation but involved an intense journey of self-discovery and personal growth. As she rebuilt her life, Lisa found new interests and passions that had been suppressed. Her story encapsulates the idea that liberation from toxic dynamics can lead to significant personal transformation, encouraging others in similar situations to believe in their inner strength.

William's experience illustrates a powerful transition from dependence to independence, exemplifying how reclaiming personal agency can lead to fulfillment. For years, William lived under the constraints of a relationship where his partner controlled many aspects of his life, from finances to social interactions. The realization that he had become a shadow of himself propelled William to make a change. He began by reevaluating his priorities, slowly regaining control over his own decisions. Enrolling in courses and pursuing hobbies, William discovered talents he never knew he possessed. This newfound independence not only redefined his identity but also provided a sense of purpose and accomplishment. His journey is a testimony to the fulfillment achieved through autonomy, offering hope to those who feel stifled in dependent relationships.

Maria's healing process highlights the transformative power of self-love and the importance of setting boundaries. After enduring years of emotional neglect,

Maria reached a breaking point. Through faith and a supportive community, she learned to value herself beyond the role she played in her relationship. Embracing self-love meant forgiving herself for past mistakes and understanding that her needs were valid. Setting boundaries became a vital practice, allowing Maria to establish healthier connections with others. Her church community played a significant role, providing affirmations of her worth and reinforcing her spiritual beliefs. Maria's journey demonstrates how faith and community can foster a nurturing environment that promotes healing and empowerment. Her story encourages others to cultivate self-love and respect, reminding them that they deserve kindness and compassion first and foremost from themselves.

John's path highlights the crucial role of spiritual practices such as prayer and meditation in post-abuse recovery. Having experienced manipulation and emotional abuse, John found solace in spirituality. Daily meditation sessions helped him reconnect with his emotions, fostering a deeper understanding of his mental state. Prayer became a tool for seeking guidance and building resilience, aiding him in processing traumatic experiences. These practices provided John with an anchor, contributing significantly to his emotional stability. Over time, he developed coping mechanisms that empowered him to navigate life's challenges with greater clarity and peace. John's story underscores the importance of incorporating spiritual practices into recovery processes, illustrating their potential to promote emotional health and resilience. His journey offers a model for integrating spirituality as a source of strength and healing, serving as a beacon for those recovering from similar circumstances.

Lessons Learned from Adversity

Overcoming toxic relationships can be one of life's most challenging yet profoundly transformative experiences. For many individuals, surviving such a tumultuous chapter marks the beginning of a journey towards emotional resilience and personal growth. This process isn't merely about leaving behind a negative environment but also involves learning to thrive in healthier conditions.

When faced with adversity, emotional resilience is forged through enduring and overcoming challenges. It acts as a vital component in developing character, shaping an individual's ability to cope with future obstacles. According to research, building resilience doesn't happen overnight; it requires reflection on past experiences and the courage to confront painful truths (Malhotra, 2024). Those who have navigated the murky waters of toxic relationships often emerge with a heightened strength, better equipped to handle life's ups and downs. They learn to approach problems not with despair but with determination, seeing each hurdle as an opportunity for growth rather than a setback.

In addition to resilience, understanding the value of self-respect is crucial in the healing journey. Recognizing personal worth independent of others' perceptions empowers individuals to set boundaries and prioritize their needs. This newfound respect begins from within, often nurtured by daily affirmations and celebrating small victories as significant achievements. These practices foster a healthier self-image and help dismantle the negative self-perceptions instilled by previous toxic dynamics (Brenner, 2024).

Being able to recognize red flags is another valuable lesson learned from escaping toxicity. Ingraining awareness of these warning signs—such as disregard for boundaries or persistent disrespect—protects individuals from falling into similar patterns in future relationships. Developing this skill is an act of self-preservation that encourages proactive behavior, enabling people to make informed decisions about who they allow into their lives. Establishing clear guidelines for what constitutes acceptable behavior fosters safer, more respectful relationships moving forward.

In non-toxic environments, individuals learn to appreciate the significance of community support networks. Surviving a harmful relationship can often leave a person feeling isolated and vulnerable, making the role of these networks indispensable. Friends, family, and support groups offer more than just a listening ear—they provide encouragement, mutual understanding, and a sense of belonging that aid significantly in recovery. Their presence reaffirms that no one has to go through this journey alone, creating a safety net that individuals can rely on during trying times.

Furthermore, integrating oneself into a supportive community nurtures the healing process by fostering human connections. These connections inspire confidence and trust, opening channels for shared experiences and mutual healing. Such environments empower individuals to explore new interests and rediscover old passions, contributing positively to one's self-esteem and identity. Some find comfort and a sense of purpose in helping others who face similar struggles, transforming personal pain into compassion and empathy.

The journey to recovery and self-discovery after leaving a toxic relationship is deeply personal and often layered with complex emotions. It's about regaining control over one's life, rebuilding self-worth, and ensuring the lessons learned pave the way for healthier future interactions. The narratives of those who've triumphed serve as a beacon of hope, illustrating that with the right strategies and support systems, it's possible to overcome even the most challenging circumstances.

Inspirational Biblical Comparisons

In the face of toxic relationships, personal stories of triumph serve as beacons of hope and resilience. Just as many individuals have faced daunting challenges, so too do biblical narratives provide timeless insights into overcoming adversity with unwavering faith and courage.

The story of the Prodigal Son offers a profound lesson in redemption and forgiveness. In this narrative, a young man squanders his inheritance and reaches a point of desperation before deciding to return home. Instead of facing rejection, he is welcomed back by his father with open arms. This tale beautifully mirrors the journey of those who have emerged from toxic relationships and found healing through forgiveness. Letting go of past hurts can be a pivotal step in one's growth, offering a chance for renewal and self-discovery. The act of forgiving oneself and others allows individuals to move beyond the shadows of their past and embrace new beginnings.

Similarly, the story of David and Goliath embodies the strength needed to confront and overcome seemingly insurmountable challenges. David, a young shepherd, faces the giant warrior Goliath armed only with a sling and five smooth stones. His victory is not just a testament to physical prowess but an affirmation of deep-rooted faith and courage. For those emerging from toxic environments, this story serves as a powerful symbol that inner strength and belief can conquer even the most intimidating obstacles. Facing toxic challenges may seem daunting, yet with faith as a cornerstone, triumph becomes attainable.

The tale of Ruth exemplifies loyalty and resilience as she stands by her mother-in-law Naomi during a time of great loss and uncertainty. Leaving her homeland, Ruth embarks on a journey filled with hardship, yet her unwavering dedication and perseverance lead to a newfound community and a bright future. This narrative highlights the importance of remaining steadfast and resilient when navigating new beginnings after a toxic relationship. Embracing change and uncertainty with loyalty to oneself and loved ones can pave the way to healing and hope. Ruth's story inspires individuals to trust in the process of rebuilding their lives, encouraging them to tackle challenges with determination.

Esther's courageous stand against injustice illustrates the power of advocacy and taking action in the face of wrongdoing. As queen, she risks her life to save her people from annihilation, embodying bravery and selflessness. Esther's narrative is a poignant reminder that confronting toxicity requires courage and the willingness to stand up for what is right. Her bold actions inspire those trapped in toxic relationships to advocate for themselves and others, breaking free from the chains of fear and oppression. By harnessing inner strength and seeking justice, individuals can navigate toward a path of empowerment and healing.

Reflecting on these biblical tales, it becomes evident that their enduring themes resonate deeply with the struggles faced by those in toxic relationships. Each story provides valuable lessons, illustrating that adversity, while challenging, also holds the potential for profound growth and transformation. The common thread running through these narratives is a call to action—whether through forgiveness, faith, resilience, or courage—that encourages individuals to rise above their circumstances.

Just as the Prodigal Son's homecoming speaks to the power of forgiveness, so does it teach the value of self-acceptance. Forgiving oneself for past mistakes is a crucial step in breaking free from toxic ties and embracing a brighter future. Similarly, adopting the determined mindset of David can empower individuals to face and conquer their own giants, no matter how daunting they may seem. Ruth's loyalty reveals the strength found in supportive relationships and communities, reminding readers of the importance of surrounding themselves with positive influences.

Furthermore, Esther's valor emphasizes the significance of standing united against wrongs, whether personal or communal. By doing so, individuals can foster environments where healing and resilience thrive, creating spaces where personal stories of triumph can flourish.

Final Thoughts

Throughout this chapter, we've explored the transformative journeys of individuals who have bravely overcome toxic relationships. Each personal story captures the essence of resilience and the pursuit of a healthier life. From Lisa's courageous steps towards freedom to William's journey from dependency to independence, we witness the profound impact of reclaiming one's agency. Maria and John's paths highlight the power of self-love and spirituality in healing, showing us that true recovery involves not just leaving behind a toxic environment but discovering our inner strengths. These stories are beacons of hope, encouraging everyone facing similar challenges to believe in their capacity for change and growth.

As we reflect on these narratives, it's essential to recognize the common thread of support and community woven throughout each experience. Whether through supportive friends, encouraging faith communities, or newfound passions, those who have triumphed over toxicity remind us of the vital importance of connection and empathy in the healing process. For individuals seeking guidance or for Christian counselors aiding others, these stories offer inspiration rooted in real-life experiences. They serve as a testament to the strength found in unity and the powerful transformation that arises when individuals refuse to let adversity define them. By embracing these lessons, we can all find the courage to create healthier, more fulfilling lives.

Chapter Ten
Restoration and Forgiveness

R estoration and forgiveness form a profound journey of personal healing, holding the potential to transform lives weighed down by past hurt. The essence of restoration lies in its ability to mend broken spirits and foster renewed hope. Forgiveness acts as the key to unlocking this transformation by releasing the heavy burdens of resentment and opening pathways to peace. In this chapter, readers will be invited to embark on an insightful exploration of these themes, uncovering the steps necessary to navigate the intricate emotional landscapes of conflict and reconciliation. Through narratives deeply anchored in empathy, you will find encouragement to seek out the courage and strength that lie in vulnerability.

Within these pages, we delve into the nuances of acknowledging pain and communicating openly as vital components of the reconciliation process. You will discover how setting realistic expectations and seeking support can guide you through the complexities of forgiveness, offering both emotional and spiritual renewal. These stories will illuminate the power of authentic expression and shared experiences as avenues toward deeper connections with others, validating the strength found in community and empathy. From practical communication techniques to insights on the delicate balance of maintaining personal boundaries, this chapter provides a comprehensive framework for those yearning for both individual healing and relational harmony, emphasizing that while forgiveness often begins within, it can lead to profound external transformations.

Steps to Personal Reconciliation

In the journey of healing and reconciliation, acknowledging the hurt is the crucial first step. When mired in the throes of conflict or betrayal, it often feels easier to suppress or ignore pain rather than face its rawness head-on. However, recognizing and owning this personal pain is vital for identifying specific grievances that obstruct reconciliation. By consciously acknowledging these emotions, you pave the way for a deeper understanding of not only your responses but also what exactly needs healing. This process might involve introspection or journaling, where you allow yourself to express emotions freely without judgment. Allowing feelings to surface and confronting them can shed light on hidden wounds, facilitating more genuine healing.

As essential as acknowledging hurt is, communicating openly with those involved forms the bridge to reconciliation. Honest conversations offer a platform to express feelings, clarify misunderstandings, and gain valuable insights into the experiences and perceptions of others. For many, engaging in these dialogues might seem daunting; fear of confrontation or vulnerability often stands in the way. Yet, true reconciliation thrives on these open channels of communication. It's in these spaces that individuals can share their truths, listen to one another with empathy, and begin to untangle the web of miscommunications that may have previously fueled discord. Techniques such as active listening and "I" statements can foster a more productive exchange, where each person feels heard and respected, laying the groundwork for mutual understanding and healing.

Moreover, realistic expectations are integral in managing this restorative journey. It's critical to recognize reconciliation as a gradual, often non-linear process. While the desire for instant resolution or forgiveness is natural, setting too high or immediate expectations can lead to disappointment and disillusionment. Instead, embracing a gradual approach allows room for setbacks and acknowledges the time necessary for genuine healing. By setting achievable milestones that honor both individual and relational progress, motivation remains sustained. Practicing patience and self-compassion can help maintain balance between aspirations for healing and the reality of emotional complexities.

Seeking forgiveness represents yet another facet of healing, offering paths towards emotional and spiritual renewal. The act of seeking forgiveness—whether from oneself, God, or others—can be profoundly liberating. It is an acknowledgment of mistakes or wrongdoings and an expression of willingness to change. This step necessitates humility and courage, allowing one to engage with the past while committing to personal growth. In Christian contexts, forgiveness aligns with scriptural teachings emphasizing love, grace, and redemption (Relationships, 2024). It's about releasing resentment and bitterness, thereby making space for new beginnings. As the Bible says, forgiving those who trespass against us is not just a religious duty but a testament to inner strength and conviction.

Therapeutic support can often facilitate these steps, offering safe environments for processing complex emotions like guilt, shame, or anger (Agius, 2024). Whether through individual counseling or family therapy, these spaces provide invaluable guidance, helping navigate feelings and reinforcing the importance of boundaries and self-care. Therapists can offer tools to reframe situations, challenge limiting beliefs, and build strategies for handling similar challenges in the future. Engaging in therapy doesn't symbolize weakness but rather reflects a proactive step toward reclaiming emotional well-being and nurturing healthier relationships.

Understanding that forgiveness does not always equate to reconciliation further emphasizes the nuanced journey of healing. Forgiveness often occurs within, freeing individuals from negative emotions without necessarily restoring previous relational dynamics. There are circumstances where maintaining boundaries proves crucial to sustaining one's safety and health. In cases involving abuse or ongoing harm, reconciliation might not be advisable, underscoring the importance of honoring personal values and boundaries over societal pressures to reconcile (Agius, 2024).

Couples or family therapy can equally be influential in pinpointing methods to repair relationship ruptures exacerbated by betrayal or conflict. These sessions emphasize developing effective communication skills and rebuilding trust through structured exercises designed to promote transparency and mutual commitment to emotional well-being. Through joint efforts coupled with individual growth, individuals learn to foster empathy and understanding, ultimately working toward a reconciliatory process tailored to their unique context.

Finding Strength in Vulnerability

Vulnerability often carries a negative connotation, perceived as a weakness in a world that values strength and resilience. Yet, embracing vulnerability can be transformative, offering a profound source of personal strength during the healing journey. At its core, vulnerability is about being authentic—allowing ourselves to be seen as we truly are, without masks or defenses.

Authenticity invites deeper connections with others, reassuring us that being vulnerable is not only acceptable but admirable. When we allow our genuine selves to emerge, we create opportunities for meaningful relationships. Authenticity reassures us and those around us that vulnerability is a testament to inner strength rather than a shortcoming (admin, 2024). It can be difficult to step into this space, particularly when societal pressures implore us to present only our best selves. Yet, by embracing our true nature, we foster environments where real connections can flourish.

In this process, sharing personal stories plays a pivotal role. By opening up about our experiences—both triumphs and trials—we build a sense of community. Personal storytelling is a bridge, connecting individuals through shared experiences and emotions. These narratives encourage mutual support, reminding us that we are not alone in our journeys. Each story we share builds a richer tapestry of understanding and empathy among us.

Empathy, in turn, is a powerful catalyst for healing. When we understand and acknowledge the shared human experience, we nurture better relationships. Nurturing these connections allows us to extend compassion to ourselves and to others. Seeing life from another's perspective fosters patience, compassion, and understanding (Alam, 2023).

Embracing vulnerability also entails recognizing the importance of accepting help from those around us. In acknowledging our need for support, we establish an essential network for recovery. This network becomes a foundation upon which we can lean during challenging times. Reaching out and allowing others into our lives demonstrates true courage. Accepting assistance or guidance shows trust and humility, inviting others to become a part of our healing journey.

The act of accepting help reflects the strength found in community and connection. It is within these circles of support that we can find resilience and rejuvenation. Encouraging others to walk alongside us on our path reminds us that we are never truly alone. The networks we form enrich our lives, providing the strength needed to face adversities with renewed vigor.

Indeed, vulnerability requires courage. It means putting aside fears of judgment and rejection, daring to step into the unknown without guarantees of acceptance. Yet, the rewards of this openness are immeasurable. It is through vulnerability that we discover our most profound strengths—our capacity for love, empathy, and understanding. And in expressing our authentic selves, we inspire others to do the same, creating a ripple effect of healing and empowerment throughout communities.

For individuals seeking emotional, mental, or spiritual healing, embracing vulnerability offers a path toward liberation from toxic bonds. It allows them to shed the weight of pretenses and step into a more fulfilling existence rooted in truth and authenticity. Vulnerability can transform pain into growth, fostering resilience and igniting the journey toward personal restoration.

Christian counselors and support group leaders may find encouraging vulnerability within their communities a powerful tool. By creating spaces where individuals feel safe to express themselves openly, they help nurture environments conducive to healing. Such relationships built on trust and empathy reinforce the community's fabric, promoting a healthier collective psyche.

Role of Forgiveness in Self-Healing

Understanding that forgiveness is a journey is crucial for personal healing and restoration. This process often involves navigating through a labyrinth of conflicting emotions, each step forward leading you closer to emotional freedom. Forgiveness is not an instantaneous decision but rather a gradual unfolding of inner resilience. It requires patience and self-compassion as one grapples with emotions like anger, sadness, and betrayal.

Research highlights the importance of addressing these emotions for forgiveness to promote healing effectively. Unforgiveness can be fueled by unresolved anger, leading to negative health effects such as stress and depression (Berry et al., 2005; Kim et al., 2022). Recognizing forgiveness as a journey allows individuals to acknowledge their feelings without being overwhelmed by them, creating space to heal and grow.

Choosing forgiveness is also a powerful act of self-liberation from the burdens of resentment. Holding onto past grievances can feel like carrying a heavy load, inhibiting personal growth and happiness. As individuals decide to forgive, they release themselves from this burden, allowing room for peace and newfound freedom. Empirical studies affirm that forgiveness correlates positively with physical and psychological health (Lee & Enright, 2019).

Moreover, reframing forgiveness as a choice rather than an obligation enhances its transformative power. Seeing it this way positions forgiveness as something within the forgiver's control, thus empowering them. Instead of feeling pressured to forgive, understanding it as a choice makes the act more genuine and meaningful. This perspective shift benefits the forgiver significantly, altering how they engage with their emotions and interact with those who have wronged them. It transforms forgiveness from a duty into a personal tool for healing and self-betterment.

When incorporating forgiveness into daily life, embracing the idea that it's a choice offers autonomy and fosters a sense of agency. This shift allows individuals to weigh their readiness and approach forgiveness in a manner that aligns with their values and emotional state. By choosing when and how to forgive, individuals can experience empowerment rather than coercion, making the journey more aligned with their personal growth and healing.

The spiritual aspect of forgiveness also plays a vital role in its acceptance as a path to peace. Scriptural teachings often advocate forgiveness as a moral virtue and route to spiritual serenity. For individuals guided by biblical teachings, these spiritual elements offer additional motivation to embrace forgiveness. Such teachings encourage believers to pursue forgiveness as a way to achieve inner peace and fulfill spiritual principles, reinforcing the idea that forgiving others aligns with broader spiritual purposes. This spiritual framework provides support and encouragement for individuals trapped in toxic relationships, offering hope and guidance through challenging times. Spiritual beliefs, therefore, become a source of strength, encouraging individuals to seek peace through forgiveness.

Incorporating spirituality into the forgiveness process not only supports personal healing but also strengthens the connection to one's faith. Believing that forgiveness serves a higher purpose can instill a deeper sense of fulfillment and tranquility. This connection between spirituality and forgiveness nurtures emotional resilience, helping individuals navigate life's adversities with grace and stability.

Recognizing the intersection of these dimensions in forgiveness—understanding it as a journey, a form of self-release, a chosen path, and a spiritual endeavor—provides a comprehensive framework for exploring its potential to reform one's life. This multifaceted view empowers individuals to take ownership of their forgiveness journey, fostering both personal recovery and spiritual growth.

It's important to highlight the significant impact that forgiveness has on reducing negative emotions and promoting overall wellbeing. The literature suggests that forgiveness therapy and similar interventions lead to reductions in anger, anxiety, and depression (Lin et al., 2004; Hansen et al., 2009). By letting go of grudges, individuals can foster a sense of hope and self-confidence, contributing to positive mental health.

Moreover, incorporating tools like mindfulness and empathy can enhance the ability to forgive. Mindfulness helps individuals observe their emotions without judgment, promoting psychological distancing from negative experiences. This practice aids in shifting perspectives, making it easier to understand and process hurtful events objectively. Similarly, empathy allows individuals to relate to others' experiences, facilitating compassion and easing the pathway towards forgiveness.

Final Thoughts

Throughout this chapter, we've navigated the intricate path of healing and forgiveness, essential for personal restoration. Acknowledging pain initiates the journey, setting the stage for understanding and healing while fostering open communication as a bridge to reconciliation. We've explored the importance of realistic expectations, recognizing that healing unfolds gradually. A step marked by humility and courage is seeking forgiveness—liberating both emotionally and spiritually. It's crucial to understand that forgiveness may not always mean reconciliation, especially in harmful relationships, where maintaining boundaries respects one's values and safety. Therapy and support play pivotal roles, offering guidance and tools to manage complex emotions, reaffirming self-care and healthy boundaries.

Embracing vulnerability emerges as a profound strength, inviting authenticity and deeper connections. It's about sharing our genuine selves, creating a tapestry of shared stories that build empathy and understanding. Accepting help forms networks of support vital for resilience. Forgiveness transforms from a burden into liberation, promoting peace within. Choosing forgiveness, seen as an empowering act rather than a duty, aligns with spiritual pathways encouraging inner peace and broader purpose. Encompassing forgiveness as a journey, a choice, and a spiritual endeavor amplifies its potential to heal and reform lives, nurturing both personal recovery and spiritual growth.

Chapter Eleven
Walking Away with God

Walking away with God means embarking on a spiritual journey that embraces change and leaves toxicity behind. It's about finding the courage to step beyond familiar boundaries while holding one's faith close, allowing divine love and wisdom to guide each step. Throughout our lives, we encounter relationships and situations that can cloud our vision and hinder our growth. Yet, with faith as our anchor, we move towards new beginnings, seeking the life God intends for us. This path may have uncertainties, but trusting in a higher power inspires confidence and renewal. Each decision to leave behind what harms us paves the way for profound self-discovery, creating space for healing and spiritual growth amidst life's transitions.

This chapter delves into the dynamic interplay between leaving toxic environments and maintaining one's faith. It explores how embracing change becomes an opportunity for personal transformation and deeper connection with God. Through narratives and biblical teachings, readers will find encouragement to trust in divine timing, viewing obstacles as stepping stones rather than barriers. The insights shared will highlight how breaking free from negativity aligns with God's greater purpose, providing individuals with strength and hope. By focusing on gratitude, prayer, and community support, this chapter offers guidance for those seeking liberation from toxic relationships, emphasizing how such steps lead to spiritual empowerment and fulfillment.

Embracing New Life Chapters

Seeing new beginnings as gifts from God can be transformative, urging us to embrace life with gratitude and hope. Often, the struggles we face in toxic situations cloud our vision of what lies ahead. Yet, seeing each new chapter as a divine gift helps to shift this perspective. One's journey might resemble a book filled with unexpected turns, yet every page turned is an opportunity for growth and renewal. It's crucial to view these changes, not as disruptions, but as essential steps towards healing and development.

Recognizing new opportunities is akin to opening a gift; it requires anticipation and trust. The challenges before us are stepping stones, not stumbling blocks, shaping our path forward. They inspire gratitude when viewed through the lens of God's love and promise, bringing hope where despair once dwelt. As highlighted in personal stories and shared experiences, trusting in God's direction offers comfort amidst uncertainty (Butterfly, 2023). Realizing that life's plan is intricately woven by a higher power empowers individuals to accept changes and welcome them with open hearts.

One cannot underestimate the importance of stepping out of comfort zones for personal and spiritual growth. Staying within familiar boundaries often hinders progress, trapping us in cycles of negativity and stagnation. By venturing beyond these self-imposed limits, we pave the way for transformation, which is vital for overcoming toxic relationships and fostering new beginnings. Embracing change challenges us to develop resilience and adaptability. This journey may feel daunting, but it's necessary for uncovering one's true potential and strengthening faith.

Engaging in activities or pursuing dreams that once seemed unattainable can lead to profound personal discoveries. Taking these leaps demonstrates courage and faith in God's greater purpose for our lives. It empowers individuals to grow spiritually, fostering deeper connections with the divine and nurturing inner strength. For those feeling trapped in toxicity, breaking free can reveal untapped talents and aspirations waiting to blossom. It opens doors to opportunities aligned with God's plan, leading to fulfillment and joy.

Trusting that God's plans exceed our imagination requires surrender and faith. When faced with life's uncertainties, it's reassuring to remember that a loving Father orchestrates our journey with infinite wisdom. This trust provides a fresh perspective, turning obstacles into opportunities and setbacks into setups for future success (Katrina, 2024). Acknowledging that our understanding is limited allows us to place unwavering confidence in His guidance, fostering peace amid turmoil.

At times, life's hardships seem insurmountable, testing both patience and faith. However, viewing these trials through the prism of God's providence reveals hidden blessings and possibilities previously overlooked. Trusting Him calls for releasing control and embracing His timing, knowing every circumstance serves a greater purpose than we can comprehend. In doing so, we discover an expansive horizon brimming with potential, encouraging us to pursue paths that fulfill our deepest yearnings.

To recognize new opportunities as divine gifts, we must seek God's guidance actively. Praying regularly, meditating on His word, and surrounding ourselves with supportive communities strengthen our connection to His will. Listening attentively to His whispers instills clarity and discernment, guiding our steps towards meaningful pursuits. It teaches us to appreciate the present moment while eagerly anticipating the wonders ahead.

Creating a vision for the future anchored in faith empowers individuals to take bold strides towards their dreams. Visualizing success and setting goals aligned with God's purpose fosters motivation and determination. Writing down aspirations and mapping actionable steps cultivates focus and perseverance, ensuring progress despite challenges. Moreover, sharing this vision with trusted allies invites encouragement and accountability, reinforcing one's commitment to growth.

Letting go of fear becomes essential in this process, for fear often paralyzes progress and stifles potential. To flourish, one must release apprehensions and doubts, replacing them with confidence in God's unwavering presence. Practicing daily affirmations and engaging in positive self-talk nurture a mindset of abundance, dispelling negativity and inspiring hope. Remember, He walks beside us every step, providing strength and assurance.

Building a Stronger Faith Foundation

In the midst of life's transitions, reinforcing one's faith can be a beacon of hope and strength. Change, although daunting, offers an opportunity to grow closer to God, to deepen spiritual practices, and to lean on the community for support and encouragement. Each step taken in faith invites divine guidance and fortification.

Deepening One's Prayer Life

One of the most profound ways to anchor faith during times of transition is through prayer. It's more than just words spoken into the void; it's an intimate dialogue with God, who knows our heartaches and desires better than we do ourselves. As stated in Romans 8:26-27, "the Spirit helps us in our weakness...the Spirit himself intercedes for us through wordless groans." This passage highlights that even when we're unsure of how to pray or what to ask for, God understands and intervenes on our behalf (Source 1). Deepening your prayer life involves creating intentional moments of stillness where you can pour out your thoughts, seek guidance, and listen for God's voice. Through this practice, individuals find solace and direction, feeling less alone in their struggles.

A practical guideline for deepening your prayer life is setting aside specific times each day solely for conversation with God. Whether morning, noon, or night, consistency builds a routine that anchors your day around God's presence. Start by expressing gratitude, then transition into sharing concerns and hopes. Conclude with silent reflection, allowing space for God's guidance to seep into your heart. Regularly incorporating scripture into your prayers can also fortify them, grounding your personal requests in the broader narrative of God's promises and wisdom.

Engaging Actively with Scripture

Beyond prayer, engaging with scripture on a deeper level provides an invaluable source of wisdom and reassurance during uncertain times. The Bible not only recounts historical transitions but also offers timeless truths applicable to modern-day challenges. For instance, Isaiah 41:10 reminds believers that God will strengthen and uphold us with His righteous right hand, offering a steadfast promise amidst turmoil (Source 2).

To truly engage with scripture, one must go beyond passive reading; it involves studying passages, reflecting on their meanings, and considering their applications to current situations. Journaling reflections and discussing insights with fellow believers are effective ways to internalize these messages. As you immerse yourself in the word, patterns of faithfulness, resilience, and redemption emerge, providing a roadmap for navigating today's uncertainties.

Developing a habit of memorizing scriptures like Joshua 1:9 ("Have I not commanded you? Be strong and courageous. Do not be frightened, and do not be dismayed, for the Lord your God is with you wherever you go.") creates a mental reservoir of hope that can be drawn upon when needed. Reciting verses aloud transforms these biblical truths into affirmations that reinforce one's faith continually.

Finding Community Among Believers

Navigating transitions is not a journey meant to be undertaken alone. Throughout biblical history, God designed us for community, knowing the strength and encouragement that arise from shared faith experiences. In Acts 2:42-47, early believers devoted themselves to fellowship and mutual support, exemplifying how community can enrich individual faith journeys.

Connecting with a group of like-minded believers provides a safe space to share struggles, celebrate victories, and hold each other accountable. Such connections are vital for those dealing with toxic relationships or seeking new beginnings. Christian counselors often emphasize the therapeutic value of community in healing processes, highlighting its role in fostering resilience and hope.

Whether participating in a small group, attending church services, or joining online faith communities, these interactions remind individuals they are part of something greater. They offer solace in the form of collective prayer, study, and worship — each aspect reinforcing the bond among believers while simultaneously strengthening the individual.

Creating opportunities for fellowship can involve organizing regular meet-ups, bible study sessions, or prayer groups. Engaging in service projects as a community not only supports others but also reinforces the sense of purpose and unity within the group. Embracing vulnerability by sharing personal experiences, both struggles and triumphs, encourages authenticity and deepens communal ties.

Practicing Gratitude

During transitions, when uncertainty looms large, practicing gratitude becomes a transformative act of faith. By intentionally recognizing and giving thanks for blessings, regardless of size, individuals shift their focus from what's lost or unknown to what remains steadfast and true.

Gratitude is intertwined with deep prayer and scripture engagement. As Philippians 4:6-7 encourages, bringing requests to God with thanksgiving leads to peace beyond understanding. These practices together cultivate an attitude of hope and trust in God's provision and timing. Reflecting on daily blessings, whether through journaling, prayer prompts, or speaking them aloud, infuses moments of light into otherwise shadowed days.

Lessons of Love and Loss Through Scripture

Understanding the transformative power of love and loss through a biblical perspective offers a profound insight into nurturing one's spiritual journey. God's steadfast love serves as an exemplary model for developing healthy relationships. The Bible often illustrates the depths of divine love, which is unwavering, patient, and forgiving. In 1 Corinthians 13:4-7, love is described as kind, not envious or boastful, a sentiment that echoes Jesus' own teachings about love. By emulating this form of love, individuals can cultivate relationships that reflect genuine care and understanding, steering clear of toxicity.

Furthermore, embracing loss, although challenging, has the potential to propel spiritual growth and ignite renewed perspectives. According to Christian teachings, loss is not merely an end but a transition that brings one closer to God's purpose. The story of Job in the Old Testament vividly portrays this idea. Despite immense suffering and loss, Job's faith remained unshaken, ultimately leading to a deeper understanding of his relationship with God. His journey underscores how enduring loss with faith can refine an individual's spiritual identity and open their eyes to new dimensions of life.

On a similar note, recognizing change as part of God's will can bring liberation and resilience. Change, often perceived as daunting, is a necessity within the journey of faith. In Ecclesiastes 3:1, it is written, "There is a time for everything, and a season for every activity under the heavens." This passage highlights the natural ebb and flow of life orchestrated by divine wisdom. Accepting change with grace transforms it into a liberating force, freeing individuals from the bonds of fear and uncertainty. When faced with change, believers are encouraged to lean on their faith, finding strength in the belief that God's plans are ultimately for their good (Jeremiah 29:11).

Through these transformations—embracing love, navigating loss, and accepting change—believers find themselves more aligned with their spiritual path. The narrative of Ruth exemplifies this beautifully. After losing her husband, Ruth clings to her mother-in-law

Naomi, declaring her loyalty not just to Naomi but also to Naomi's God (Ruth 1:16). Her decision to leave behind her past signifies a powerful shift towards embracing new beginnings predestined by God. Ruth's story culminates in her becoming an ancestor to King David, illustrating how adherence to faith amidst change can lead to unexpected blessings and legacies.

In practicing God's enduring love, individuals build bridges of compassion and empathy in their relationships, avoiding the traps of bitterness and resentment. As outlined in Ephesians 4:2, followers of Christ are called to "be completely humble and gentle; be patient, bearing with one another in love." This approach to relationships fosters environments where healing takes precedence over hurt, paving the way for healthier interactions grounded in mutual respect and kindness.

Moreover, confronting loss in the light of faith encourages personal introspection and spiritual enlightenment. Loss challenges individuals to reevaluate their priorities, teaching them to relinquish superficial attachments and focus on everlasting values. The Apostle Paul, in Philippians 3:8, shares that he considers everything a loss compared to the surpassing worth of knowing Christ. His transformation from a persecutor of Christians to a devoted apostle provides a testament to how grappling with loss can redefine one's core beliefs and aspirations.

Finally, perceiving change as an essential facet of divine will empowers believers to rise above adversities with unwavering resiliency. In Romans 12:2, Christians are urged not to conform to the patterns of this world, but to be transformed by the renewing of their minds. This renewal, sparked by acceptance of divine change, equips individuals with the courage to embrace new chapters in their lives, fortified by faith and trust in God's omnipotence.

This intricate interplay between love, loss, and change weaves a tapestry of divine orchestration that guides believers toward enriched spiritual experiences. Through love, they learn to nurture and cherish connections that mirror God's benevolence. Through loss, they undergo cleansing metamorphoses that distill their spirits. And through change, they forge paths of liberation and hope, resiliently marching forward in their journey with God.

Pastor Timothy Tomlinson, in his sermon series on healing, emphasizes how Jesus' teachings guide individuals through emotional turmoil, offering the promise of peace and restoration. Just as Elizabeth found solace and renewal in Christ's love during her struggles, others too can embrace these biblical lessons for transformative personal growth (Tomlinson, 2024).

In pursuing these teachings, believers find the assurance that they do not walk alone. Instead, they tread each step strengthened by faith, enveloped in divine love, and attuned to the ever-evolving melody of life orchestrated by God.

Final Insights

The chapter has delved into the profound journey of leaving behind toxic environments while holding onto faith as a guiding beacon. It has explored how viewing new beginnings as divine gifts can shift perspectives from despair to hope, inviting spiritual growth and transformation. By stepping out of comfort zones, individuals can overcome negative cycles and embrace change with resilience and adaptability. The process, while daunting, unveils hidden talents and renewed purpose, aligning their lives with God's greater plan. Through engaging actively in prayer and scripture, believers fortify their connection to divine wisdom, finding solace and direction amid life's uncertainties.

Engaging with these teachings encourages personal and spiritual development, reminding us that we're never alone in our journeys. Change, loss, and love are intricately interwoven, offering rich lessons for those seeking healing and renewal from toxicity. By nurturing relationships grounded in empathy and reflecting God's benevolence, individuals foster healthier connections. Embracing loss with faith guides them towards deeper introspection, while acceptance of change empowers them with courage and hope. This chapter invites readers to seek God's guidance actively, trusting that His plans exceed human understanding and holding fast to the promise of new, fulfilling paths ahead.

Chapter Twelve
Conclusion

In the journey toward healing from toxic relationships, the first critical step is awareness. It's vital to recognize the behaviors that undermine our sense of self and distort our perception of love. Understanding these signs not only safeguards our emotional well-being but also empowers us to address the reality we often try to ignore. It's like peeling away layers of denial that have encased us in false security. Identifying the recurring need for validation or the subtle manipulations that leave us questioning our worth are signs we can no longer afford to dismiss.

Take, for instance, the feeling of constantly walking on eggshells, contemplating every word before speaking, fearing reproach or cold silence. This is not a requirement of love; it's a symptom of toxic behavior. Recognizing such patterns requires honesty with oneself, sometimes painfully so. It involves admitting that perhaps what was perceived as love could have been control or conditional affection. Empowerment begins here, at this juncture of painful truth, because once you see the situation for what it is, you possess the power to change it.

With awareness comes the necessity of setting boundaries, an essential tool for those ready to reclaim their lives. Boundaries act as the protective walls around our hearts and souls, defining what behaviors we will accept and what we must repudiate. They are not prisons keeping people out, but rather guidelines ensuring mutual respect and understanding. Think of boundaries as personal guidelines helping us navigate relationships with confidence and clarity.

The process of establishing these boundaries might be fraught with challenges and misunderstanding, particularly when faced with a person resistant to change. However, being assertive about your needs and limits is not just a declaration of self-worth, but also an invitation for others to follow suit. Setting boundaries doesn't mean erecting insurmountable walls; it means creating spaces where respect can thrive. This assertion of self-respect reinforces our identity, fortifying our emotional armor against manipulation or guilt.

Parallel to boundary-setting is the transformative power of forgiveness. Often misunderstood, forgiveness is not about excusing the wrongs done to us or inviting past hurts back into our lives. Rather, it serves as a gift to oneself—a release from the chains of resentment and anger. Forgiving those who have wronged us can be one of the most liberating and healing actions we take. It's about saying "I refuse to let your actions hold power over my emotions any longer."

Forgiveness allows us to move forward without the heavy baggage of bitterness weighing us down. It's an act that refocuses our energies on our own healing journey instead of fixating on the transgressions of others. Realize, though, that forgiving does not demand reconciliation nor does it imply forgetting. It's more a conscious decision to embrace peace over turmoil, letting go of corrosive sentiments that hinder growth and happiness.

While individual transformation is significant, healing can be profoundly enriched by embracing community support. Nobody should have to face the aftermath of toxic relationships alone. Engaging with a community offers connection and shared experiences that remind us we're not isolated in our struggles. Sharing stories within supportive groups lays bare a testament to human capacity for resilience and renewal.

There is undeniable strength in numbers—strength in knowing there are others who genuinely understand the depths of your pain because they have walked a similar path. This kinship provides an unparalleled sense of belonging. It assures us that while our paths might be difficult, there is always hope for better days. Compassionate communities serve as beacons of encouragement, guiding us through periods of darkness towards the light of restoration.

For Christian counselors and support group leaders, nurturing these communities becomes paramount. Providing safe spaces where individuals can express their truths without judgment fosters healing atmospheres. Equipping these communities with biblical teachings centered on love, patience, and kindness reinforces spiritual recovery. Facilitating conversations rooted in empathy, where advice is gently given not as prescriptions but offerings of solidarity, can uplift struggling spirits significantly.

As we close this journey together, reflect on the divine promise of renewal and grace. Approach each day with a renewed commitment to live authentically and joyfully, surrounded by individuals who value and support you. Let your heart remain open to receiving love that honors your soul, grounded in the truth that you are worthy of healthy relationships.

Embarking on the path towards healing toxic wounds is not easy, yet it promises profound growth, freedom, and ultimately, joy. You owe it to yourself to break free from shackles of harmful connections and rise above adversity. Commit to surrounding yourself with positive influences, setting firm boundaries, and offering forgiveness—not as an absolution for wrongdoers but as a salve for your spirit. Embrace support from those who understand, because healing, though deeply personal, flourishes in communion with others.

May your steps forward be guided by clarity, bolstered by courage, and filled with hope. As you navigate this new chapter, remember that despite the challenges along the way, you are never alone. There are countless others, buoyed by faith and community, walking beside you on this collective journey towards wholeness. Let their strength bolster yours, and know that brighter horizons await just beyond the confines of today's struggles.

Chapter Thirteen
Reference Page

Letting Go: Walking Away from Toxic Relationships
Chapter 1 - Recognizing Narcissism

Cuncic, A. (2021, November 18). *Effects of Narcissistic Abuse* . Verywell Mind. https://www.verywellmind.com/effects-of-narcissistic-abuse-5208164

Fishman, S. (2017, August 21). *Identifying and Recovering from Narcissistic Abuse* . Psych Central. https://psychcentral.com/health/signs-youre-the-victim-of-narcissistic-abuse

Ronningstam, E. (2023). *Narcissistic Personality Disorder: Guide for Providers at McLean Hospital* . Www.mcleanhospital.org; Mclean Hospital. https://www.mcleanhospital.org/npd-provider-guide

Smith, M., & Robinson, L. (2018, November 3). *Narcissistic Personality Disorder: Symptoms, Causes, Help* . HelpGuide.org. https://www.helpguide.org/mental-health/personality-disorders/narcissistic-personality-disorder

Turecki, J. (2021, June 14). *The Differences Between Healthy, Unhealthy and Toxic Relationships.* JILLIAN TURECKI. https://www.jillianturecki.com/blog/2021/6/14/the-differences-between-healthy-unhealthy-and-toxic-relationships

Welsh, T. (2023, October 13). *Unlocking Healthy Relationship Dynamics: Tips & Insights | Thriveworks* . Https://Thriveworks.com/. https://thriveworks.com/help-with/relationships/relationship-dynamics/

Chapter 2: Biblical Guidance for Freedom

14 Encouraging Verses to Give Abuse Survivors Hope - Topical Studies . (n.d.). Biblestudytools.com. https://www.biblestudytools.com/bible-study/topical-studies/encouraging-verses-to-give-abuse-survivors-hope.html

Allendale Baptist Church - How to Deal with Toxic People (A Guide for Christi . (n.d.). Allendalebaptist.org. https://allendalebaptist.org/toxic-people-christians-how-to

From Desperation to Transformation . (2020). Proverbs31.org; Proverbs 31 Ministries. https://proverbs31.org/read/devotions/full-post/2020/04/30/from-desperation-to-transformation

Freedom & Transformation Archives - Maryann Ward . (2024, October 21). Maryann Ward. https://maward.ca/category/inspirational-blog/freedom-transformation/

How healthy boundaries are more about God and other people (not me) . (2024, February 2). Wrestled Faith. https://wrestledfaith.wordpress.com/2024/02/02/how-healthy-boundaries-are-more-about-god-and-other-people-not-me/

Leight, R. (2021, June 9). *Spiritual Boundaries* . Faithbygrace.org. https://www.faithbygrace.org/spiritual-boundaries

Chapter 3: Guard Your Heart

Howard, A. H., Roberts, M., Mitchell, T., & Wilke, N. G. (2023, February 11). *The relationship between spirituality and resilience and well-being: A study of 529 care leavers from 11 nations* . Adversity and Resilience Science. https://doi.org/10.1007/s42844-023-00088-y

Manning, L., Ferris, M., Narvaez Rosario, C., Prues, M., & Bouchard, L. (2019). *Spiritual resilience: Understanding the protection and promotion of well-being in the later life* . Journal of Religion, Spirituality & Aging. https://doi.org/10.1080/15528030.2018.1532859

Manipulators and Predators are Everywhere! Discover How to Spot Red Flags and Heal from Manipulation! (2023, October 6). Drcarlamanly. https://www.drcarlamanly.com/manipulators-and-predators-are-everywhere-discover-how-to-spot-red-flags-and-heal-from-manipulation/

NERIS Analytics Limited. (2024, October 21). *Recognizing Signs of Manipulation: Advice for Vulnerable Personality Types* . 16Personalities; NERIS Analytics Limited. https://www.16personalities.com/articles/recognizing-signs-of-manipulation-advice-for-vulnerable-personality-types

Nash, J. (2018, January 5). *How to set healthy boundaries & build positive relationships* . Positive Psychology. https://positivepsychology.com/great-self-care-setting-healthy-boundaries/

Reid, S. (2022, July 6). *Setting Healthy Boundaries in Relationships - HelpGuide.org* . HelpGuide.org. https://www.helpguide.org/relationships/social-connection/setting-healthy-boundaries-in-relationships

Chapter 4: Understanding the Manipulation

Güler, A., Bankston, K., & Smith, C. R. (2022, September 13). *Self-esteem in the context of intimate partner violence: A concept analysis* . Nursing Forum. https://doi.org/10.1111/nuf.12798

Microgility. (2023, March 17). *Difference B/W Emotional and Mental Abuse: Recovery & Tips* . Faith Behaviroal Health. https://faithbehavioralhealth.com/emotional-and-mental-abuse/

Stritof, S. (2023, March 9). *Is There Manipulation in Your Marriage?* Verywell Mind. https://www.verywellmind.com/manipulation-in-marriage-2302245

What are ghosting, benching, gaslighting, and lovebombing? Tactics of emotional abuse. - Becky's Fund . (2017, August 10). Becky's Fund. https://www.beckysfund.org/ghosting-benching-gaslighting-lovebombing-tactics-emotional-abuse/

https://www.facebook.com/profile.php?id=100049200874926. (2024, February 7). *Biblical Manipulation: 10 Intriguing Examples Explored* . Scriptural Thinking. https://scripturalthinking.com/examples-of-manipulation-in-the-bible/

Chapter 5: Balancing Boundaries with Grace

Buckles, S. (2024, March 9). *What does the Bible say about toxic family members?* WisdomShort.com; WisdomShort. https://doi.org/10001864/shawn_64871_hyper_realistic_depiction_of_a_family_forging_a_pat_97f7123f-305f-4baf-92ef-26466cb76559-1400x788-crop-q90

ComplexityBeauty. (2024, October 13). *Keep Calm and Carry On: Mastering Adversity with Composure and Determination* . Medium; Thoughtscapes. https://medium.com/thoughtscapes/keep-calm-and-carry-on-mastering-adversity-with-composure-and-determination-505fdcb6cabe

How to Defend Your Boundaries and Be Assertive . (2023). Psychology Today. https://www.psychologytoday.com/intl/blog/the-wisdom-of-anger/202312/how-to-defend-your-boundaries-and-be-assertive

Harvard Professional Development. (2019). *How to improve your emotional intelligence* . Professional Development | Harvard DCE; President and Fellows of Harvard College. https://professional.dce.harvard.edu/blog/how-to-improve-your-emotional-intelligence/

Hoffman, N. (2021, April 16). *To Forgive Doesn't Automatically Mean To Reconcile* . Flying Free. https://www.flyingfreenow.com/to-forgive-doesnt-automatically-mean-to-reconcile/

Nash, J. (2018, January 5). *How to set healthy boundaries & build positive relationships* . Positive Psychology. https://positivepsychology.com/great-self-care-setting-healthy-boundaries/

Chapter 6: Healing Through Faith

Buckles, S. (2024, March 9). *What does the Bible say about toxic family members?* WisdomShort.com; WisdomShort. https://doi.org/10001864/

shawn_64871_hyper_realistic_depiction_of_a_family_forging_a_pat_97f7123f-305f-4baf-92ef-26466cb76559-1400x788-crop-q90

ComplexityBeauty. (2024, October 13). *Keep Calm and Carry On: Mastering Adversity with Composure and Determination* . Medium; Thoughtscapes. https://medium.com/thoughtscapes/keep-calm-and-carry-on-mastering-adversity-with-composure-and-determination-505fdcb6cabe

How to Defend Your Boundaries and Be Assertive . (2023). Psychology Today. https://www.psychologytoday.com/intl/blog/the-wisdom-of-anger/202312/how-to-defend-your-boundaries-and-be-assertive

Harvard Professional Development. (2019). *How to improve your emotional intelligence* . Professional Development | Harvard DCE; President and Fellows of Harvard College. https://professional.dce.harvard.edu/blog/how-to-improve-your-emotional-intelligence/

Hoffman, N. (2021, April 16). *To Forgive Doesn't Automatically Mean To Reconcile* . Flying Free. https://www.flyingfreenow.com/to-forgive-doesnt-automatically-mean-to-reconcile/

Nash, J. (2018, January 5). *How to set healthy boundaries & build positive relationships* . Positive Psychology. https://positivepsychology.com/great-self-care-setting-healthy-boundaries/

Chapter 7: Tools for Personal Growth

5 Psychology-Backed Tips to Stay Committed to Your New Year Goals - Mindstate Psychology Blog . (2024). Mindstatepsychology.com.au. https://www.mindstatepsychology.com.au/blog/how-to-stay-committed-to-new-year-goals

Alberts, H. (2024, August 31). *Charting a Path to Transformation: The Science Behind Behavior Change*

Planning . Quenza. https://quenza.com/blog/behavior-change-planning/

Paul, S. (2024, March 16). *Bridger Peaks Counseling* . Bridger Peaks Counseling. https://www.bozemancounseling.org/blog/2024/3/16/the-healing-power-of-community-understanding-its-impact-on-mental-health

Sutton, J. (2018, May 14). *5 Benefits of Journaling for Mental Health* . Positive Psychology. https://positivepsychology.com/benefits-of-journaling/

The Healing Power of Community and Connection . (2022). Psychology Today. https://www.psychologytoday.com/intl/blog/keeping-it-real-and-resilient/202204/the-healing-power-of-community-and-connection

University of Rochester Medical Center. (2019). *Journaling for Mental Health* . Rochester.edu; University of Rochester Medical Center. https://

www.urmc.rochester.edu/encyclopedia/content.aspx?ContentID=4552&ContentTypeID=1

Chapter 8: Stories of Triumph

Brenner, B. (2024, September 20). *Overcoming the Psychological Impact of Toxic Relationships: Strategies for Healing and Moving Forward* . Therapy Group of DC. https://therapygroupdc.com/therapist-dc-blog/overcoming-the-psychological-impact-of-toxic-relationships-strategies-for-healing-and-moving-forward/

Fey, T. (2024, July 9). *8 bible stories that will help you become a better person* . Bible Scripture. https://biblescripture.net/8-bible-stories-that-will-help-you-become-a-better-person/

Malhotra, W. (2024, November 8). *Healing from Toxic Relationships: Kim Peirano Of Courage to Transform On How To Survive And Thrive After Psychological Abuse* . Medium; Authority Magazine. https://

medium.com/authority-magazine/healing-from-toxic-relationships-kim-peirano-of-courage-to-transform-on-how-to-survive-and-thrive-bade4ba455aa

Metzger, D. (2024, June 26). *The One Who Struggles with God* . Literature and History Podcast. https://literatureandhistory.com/episode-019-the-one-who-struggles-with-god/

Malhotra, W. (2024, July 29). *Healing from Toxic Relationships: Barbara Martinez On How To Survive And Thrive After Psychological Abuse* . Medium. https://medium.com/@wandamalhotra/healing-from-toxic-relationships-barbara-martinez-on-how-to-survive-and-thrive-after-600a9660ae79

nohely@mypurposepursuit.com. (2018, December 23). *How a Toxic Relationship Opened Doors for Self Transformation - Thrive Global* . Thrive Global. https://community.thriveglobal.com/how-a-toxic-relationship-opened-doors-for-self-transformation/

Chapter 9: Restoration and Forgiveness

Agius, M. (2024, April 9). *Navigating the Path of Healing: Forgiveness versus Reconciliation* . Third Wave Psychotherapy. https://www.3rdwavetherapy.com/navigating-the-path-of-healing-forgiveness-versus-reconciliation/

Alam, M. A. (2023, July 17). *Embracing Vulnerability: Life Lessons in Authenticity and Connection* . Medium; ILLUMINATION. https://medium.com/illumination/embracing-vulnerability-life-lessons-in-authenticity-and-connection-1c126c078349

Kim, J. J., Payne, E. S., & Tracy, E. L. (2022, February 21). *Indirect Effects of Forgiveness on Psychological Health through Anger and Hope: a Parallel Mediation Analysis* . Journal of Religion and Health. https://doi.org/10.1007/s10943-022-01518-4

Relationships, I. (2024, March 5). *Lindsay Walden* . Lindsay Walden. https://www.lindsaywalden.com/ripples-in-communication/forgiveness-beyond-apologies-navigating-personal-growth-and-healing-in-relationships

Sutton, J. (2020, September 3). *Psychology of Forgiveness: 10+ Fascinating Research Findings* . PositivePsychology.com. https://positivepsychology.com/psychology-of-forgiveness/

admin. (2024, April). *Embracing Vulnerability: The Strength in Authenticity - Wings* . Wings. https://wingsofthefuturenfp.org/nurturing-a-compassionate-connection-with-yourself-6/

Chapter 10: Walking Away with God

Butterfly, A. L. (2023, July 18). *Nothing Can Stop God's Plan For Your Life - A Little Butterfly - Medium* .

Medium. https://medium.com/@writerbutterfly/nothing-can-stop-gods-plan-for-your-life-270bfb5328bc

Cramer, M. (2024, August 15). *Scriptures to Help Walk through Today's Transitions* . Mistycramer.com; Misty Cramer. https://www.mistycramer.com/index.php/component/k2/item/99-scriptures-to-help-walk-through-today-s-transitions

Dr. David Wolfe. (2023, July 8). *01-Transformative Power Of God's Word (Hebrews 4:1-11)* . Bensenvillebiblechurch.com. https://www.bensenvillebiblechurch.com/01-transformative-power-of-god-s-word-hebrews-4-1-11

Kristin. (2021, May 18). *The Gospel and Transitions in Life - Raising Everyday Disciples* . Raising Everyday Disciples. https://raisingeverydaydisciples.com/the-gospel-and-transitions-in-life/

Katrina. (2024, March 9). *Divine Guidance: Trusting in God's Plan for Your Life* . Medium. https://

medium.com/@katrinapaula/divine-guidance-trusting-in-gods-plan-for-your-life-514437e21a56

Tomlinson, P. T. (2024, January 19). *Journey to Healing: Embracing the Transformative Power of Jesus - Part 2* . Timothy Tomlinson. https://www.timothytomlinson.org/single-post/journey-to-healing-embracing-the-transformative-power-of-jesus-part-2

Chapter Fourteen
My Other books

1. HOW TO INFLUENCE YOUR HUSBAND TO SUCCESS (The Secrets & Keys To Becoming An Influential Wife) by Charles Brown O
2. EMBRACING EQUALITY IN MARRIAGE (Building A Togetherness That Last) By Charles O Brown
3. LETTING GO: Walking Away from Toxic Relationships. By Charles O Brown

All my books are available on Kindle and Paper Back Formats and can be purchase from all books platforms; amazon books, tiktok store for hard copy.

Printed in Dunstable, United Kingdom